QAYAQS & CANOES

Native Ways of Knowing

ALASKA NATIVE HERITAGE CENTER

Writer/Editor Jan Steinbright   Photography by Clark James Mishler

Alaska Native Heritage Center
8800 Heritage Center Drive
Anchorage, Alaska 99506

ISBN 0-9709164-0-X

Unless otherwise noted all photos
© 2001 Clark James Mishler

Historical photos courtesy Anchorage
Museum of History and Art; Alaska State
Library, Juneau; Washington State
Historical Society, Tacoma

Design by David Freeman

Prepress by Visible Ink and Norstar Color
Anchorage, Alaska
Printed by Graphic Arts Center
Portland, Oregon

Right: Toksook Bay skin kayak (center) with
hunting tools and float at dedication ceremony
at Alaska Native Heritage Center.

Cover: Northwest Coast Dugout Canoe, Siberian
Yupik Angyapik and Alutiiq Baidarka at the
launching ceremony in Homer, Alaska.

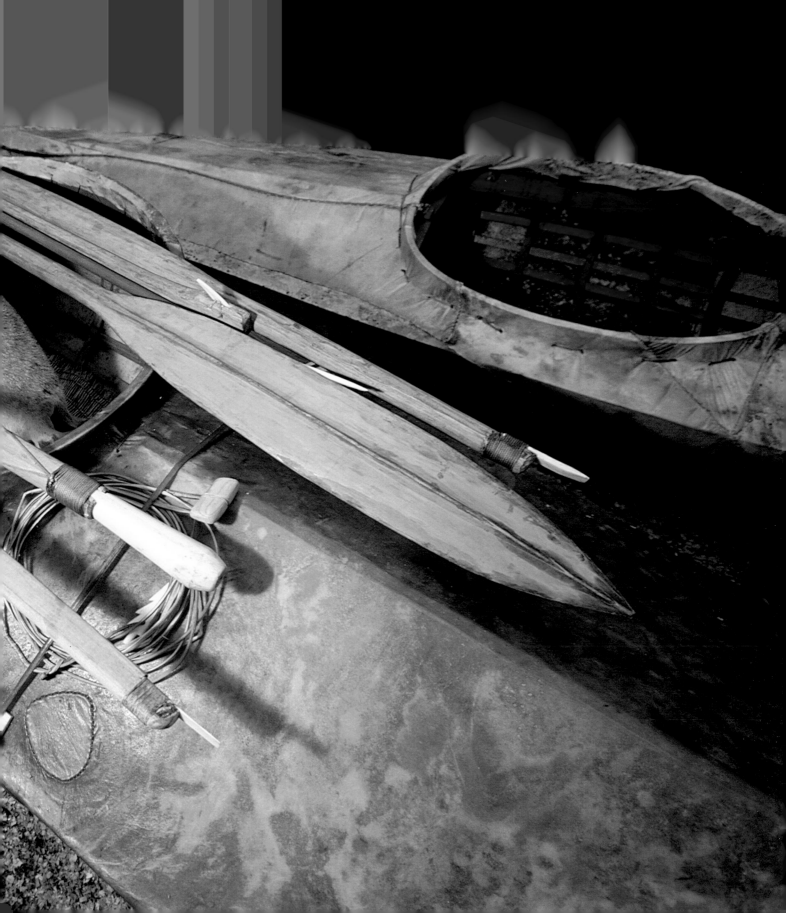

Dedication ceremony at Alaska Native Heritage Center
for completed traditional Alaska Native boats.

Contents

Map vi

Foreword vii

Preface viii

Introduction x

Bark Canoes 3

Athabascan Birch Bark Canoe, Black River Style 8

Athabascan Birch Bark Canoe 18

Kayaks 29

Central Yup'ik Qayaq, Caninermiut Style 36

Central Yup'ik Qayaq 52

Aleut (Unangan) Ulûxtax 60

Aleut Hunting Hats 74

Alutiiq (Sugpiaq) Baidarka 76

Open Skin Boats 88

Siberian Yupik Angyapik 92

Dugout Canoes 100

Northwest Coast Dugout Canoe, Northern Style 106

Notes 120

Glossary 122

References 123

Acknowledgements 124

Dedication 125

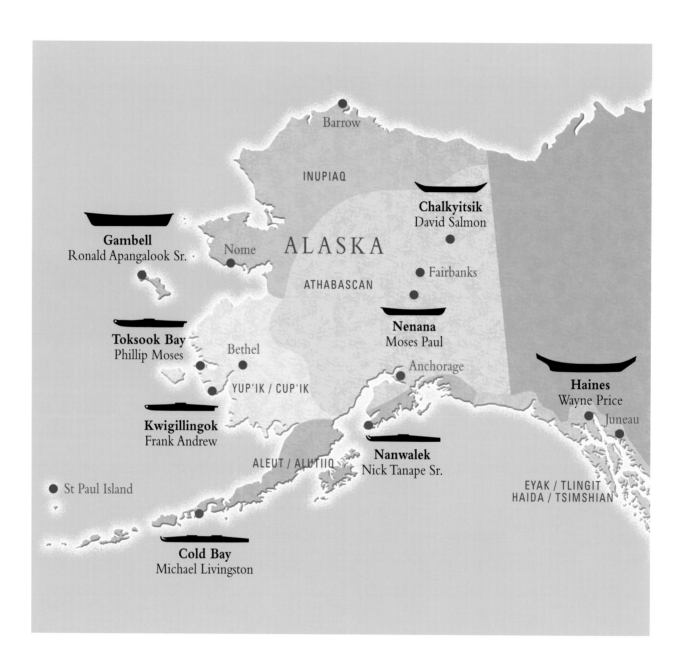

Gambell
Ronald Apangalook Sr.

Nome

INUPIAQ

Barrow

Chalkyitsik
David Salmon

ALASKA

Fairbanks

ATHABASCAN

Nenana
Moses Paul

Toksook Bay
Phillip Moses

Bethel

Anchorage

YUP'IK / CUP'IK

Haines
Wayne Price

Juneau

Kwigillingok
Frank Andrew

ALEUT / ALUTIIQ

Nanwalek
Nick Tanape Sr.

EYAK / TLINGIT
HAIDA / TSIMSHIAN

St Paul Island

Cold Bay
Michael Livingston

Foreword

We sang.

We danced.

Our hearts soared like the geese that flew overhead in the warm blue skies. This was how I felt at the fall ceremony marking the end of the year-long theme program, *Qayaqs and Canoes: Paddling into the Millennium.* During this year Alaska Native master craftsmen built eight traditional watercraft of our people. Thanks so much to Rockefeller Foundation, Save America's Treasures, National Trust for Historic Preservation, National Park Service, and Institute of Museum and Library Services for funding this program.

As I looked around the Talking Circle where I was seated with many Alaska Natives and honored guests, I saw so much pride. There were knowing smiles on everyone's face. It brought tears to my eyes.

Our Alaska Native leaders and tradition bearers, in conceiving the vision of the Center, hoped that the programs offered here would have significant meaning for Alaska Natives and our ways of life. It was hoped that the Center, over time, would strengthen the sense of pride among our people for who we are, and a sense of pride for all Alaskans alike. Also, it was hoped that this would be a place where Alaskans and others can come to understand Native ways, our values, systems and beliefs. It was hoped that through education received at the Center, all people could move toward greater understanding of each other in more positive ways.

I know that with this year's program of building these vessels we've accomplished that vision. But really, we accomplished so much more. Our lives are richer for the experiences gained here by learning from the master artisans who shared their traditional knowledge and the age-old traditions of the Alaska Native cultures.

We need these traditions, not only to know who we are, but to know who we can become.

Margaret Nelson

Margaret Nelson, a Tlingit Indian originally from Juneau, is President and CEO of the Alaska Native Heritage Center.

Preface

Over a period of five months I had the honor of being able to meet, observe and interview the tradition bearers that were invited to the Alaska Native Heritage Center to construct eight traditional Alaska Native boats. The project, *Qayaqs and Canoes: Paddling into the Millennium*, was very ambitious in scope and made history with its content. Never before had there been such an assemblage of distinct and different types of Native boats all in one place at one time. The launching ceremony took place in September in Homer as part of the Pratt Museum's semi-annual "Festival Tamanta Katwhluta." When the completed boats entered the waters of Kachemak Bay for their christening, the crowd that assembled on shore was amazed. They expressed this by exclamations and applause. What a sight! A walrus hide-covered whaling boat from the Bering Sea paddled right alongside a brightly-painted cedar dugout from Southeast. Sealskin kayaks joined a flotilla of contemporary kayaks that paddled over from Nanwalek to greet the new boats and their builders. Two birch bark canoes from the Interior quietly waited on shore, crowds gathering around them to inspect their spruce root lashings and ingenious use of bark.

The methodology I used to produce this book documenting the boat project was one of conducting taped interviews with the master boat builders, their apprentices and some of the skin sewers. As I sat and watched the building processes, I was totally absorbed by the energy that surrounded each of the construction sites. Visitors to the sites seemed to understand what a precious cultural activity they were witnessing, one that was almost a lost art to Alaska Native culture.

The taped interviews were transcribed and edited. What awaits you, the reader, is a variety of stories in the words of these gifted culture bearers. Each one has a different story to tell, but all have a common thread running through them. It is a sense of tremendous respect for their ancestors and what they accomplished. I have strived to preserve their voices and personalities in the edited versions.

You are about to embark on a cultural journey. The words contained in each of these chapters will transport you along Interior rivers and out into the stormy seas surrounding this great land called Alaska. They'll allow you to visit villages and get a glimpse of life there. But most of all, you will come to know some of the most talented and dedicated men and women. They love and honor their indigenous cultures and want to share the technologies and values their ancestors developed and passed on to them. It was through this spirit of sharing that this book was made possible.

Jan Steinbright

Jan Steinbright is a writer and an oral historian. She has worked with programs involving Alaska Native culture for more than twenty years.

Performers and onlookers at dedication ceremony
viewed through bow hole of Central Yu'pik qayaq.

Introduction

Alaska Natives are people of the tides, the rivers and the sea: maritime people. The salt and fresh waters brought food and supplies to them and provided thoroughfares for travel by boat. For centuries, their ancestors constructed watercraft to meet the moods and challenges of the southeastern coastal passages, the open oceans of the southwest and west, and the swift rivers of the Interior and north.

Before European contact, skin-covered kayaks and open angyapiks and umiaks were used in Alaska by all of the northern groups: the Aleuts of the Aleutian Chain; the Alutiiqs of Kodiak Island archipelago, Prince William Sound and outer Kenai Peninsula; the Iñupiat; Central Yup'ik; Siberian Yupik and Cup'ik.

In the Interior, bark- and skin-covered canoes answered the need for water transportation. Dugout canoes carved from a single log were the main mode of transportation in southeast Alaska.

Beaver Canoe

The critical importance of boats to the very survival of Alaska Natives is aptly illustrated by the Angoon Beaver Canoe story:

In 1882, a ship from the United States Navy bombarded the village of Angoon over a dispute. Two days prior to the bombardment, a harpoon gun on a whaling vessel operated by the Northwest Trading Company had discharged, killing a Tlingit shaman, a very important Angoon leader. He and his family had been employed by the Northwest Trading Company to direct the whalers in hunting. The relatives demanded time to grieve and blankets as compensation for his death, as was the custom. The Trading Company sent word to Sitka that the

Natives were on the warpath, not giving an explanation as to why. A U.S. Naval ship was sent to make them return the whaling boat. When the Tlingit refused and continued to demand compensation, the Navy bombed the village and destroyed all but a few houses. They also destroyed all the canoes and the food stores that had been put up during summer for the long winter ahead.

One canoe was saved, a canoe belonging to the Deisheetaan clan. It was away hunting at the time. It had a removable carved prow design of a beaver, the crest of that clan. It was taken off for safekeeping. Somehow it was lost.

During the cold winter of 1882-83 that ensued, that canoe became the main instrument of survival for the village of Angoon. It was the only means of providing food to the villagers who had taken refuge in the forest.

The canoe was held in such high esteem that years later, when it cracked and could no longer be used, it was cremated just like a person. It had come from a living thing, a great tree, and it became an instrument of survival. It was given a name and was put to rest, just as a person would be, with great respect and care.

The story of the canoe and its prow had been handed down for six generations when it reached a Tlingit man named Harold Jacobs. He was visiting the Museum of Natural History in New York as a repatriation specialist for the Tlingit-Haida Central Council when he found the beaver canoe prow. He related that when he was in the storage area of the museum, a very strong force led him down the aisle right to the beaver prow carving. As a result, this important piece of clan history has been returned to the village of Angoon and the Deisheetaan clan.[1]

History

The technology of Alaska Native boat building has been passed on for thousands of years through oral history. Nothing was written down. The young learned from the masters and, when their turn came, trained others. This pattern was severely interrupted upon contact with European civilizations. Alaska Native people were discouraged from speaking their languages and practicing traditional ceremonies. The cultural ways, including many of the technologies that had been practiced for thousands of years, began to wane. Traditional boat building was one of the technologies that suffered.

Another factor that had great influence upon this demise was the introduction of western materials and technologies. The advent of outboard motors, aluminum boats and other advances introduced with contact have resulted in the replacement of the traditional boats. These new materials provided watercraft that were sturdier and faster, making travel over long distances more readily accessible and, in some cases, hunting an easier task. The Native people, who have a long history of creative adaptation, readily accepted these advances. Sadly, these once indispensable subsistence items used by all Alaska Native people are now seen more in museums than on the hunting grounds.

Before contact with western civilizations, only natural materials were available for boat construction. Alaska Native people became extremely adept at gathering and processing raw materials. They built watertight craft using trees, skins, driftwood, bark, roots, sinew and simple hand-made tools.

Due to the fragility of these materials, little evidence in the archeological record remains today enabling us to know just how long ago some of these craft actually came into use. We have to resort to reading early exploration journals, looking at models, old photographs and early expedition sketches to see the types of boats in use. Archeological evidence dates skin-covered boats back at least 2,000 years.[2] But there is speculation that skin-covered boats were probably in use at the time the Bering Land Bridge connected present-day Alaska and Siberia.[3] Sea mammals were an important part of the indigenous peoples' diet of that region. Skin boats would have been a logical solution for transportation and hunting needs, given the local materials available.

Little has been recorded about the bark canoes for the historical record with regard to their chronological history. The material of birch bark, by its very nature, is fragile and lasts, at the most, only a few decades on a canoe frame, leaving little or no archeological evidence. This contrasts with the dugouts which could endure for at least a hundred years, especially if submerged in water. The bark canoes were seen in use by the earliest explorers to the Interior. But that record gives only a partial picture dating back to the mid-1800s. In the forty-eight contiguous states, there are some written accounts of bark canoes in journals from the mid-1700s and others from French explorers in Canada dating back as far as 1535.[4] And, there is the oral history of the Athabascan people themselves. David Salmon relates one of these stories about the first canoe maker in his interview.[5]

The dugout canoes of Southeast are included in narratives from a distant time, a time of the great stories. The members of the Kiks.ádi clan of Sitka are the caretakers of the story of the famous Kiks.ádi navigator, Kaax'achgóok, who was caught in a storm in a dugout canoe and traveled all the way from Alaska to Hawaii. After living there for some time, he and his crew made an incredible return voyage to Alaska.[6] This was at a time when Mt. Edgecumbe had ceased erupting and the snow on its peak served as a beacon for this famous voyage's return home. Volcanologists believe the mountain ceased erupting 4,000 to 4,500 years ago when two small eruptions took place. The major eruptions occurred 10,000 years ago with a hiatus between 8000 B.C. and 2500 B.C.[7] So, we know the story is, at the very least, 4,000 years old and possibly much older.

Legends from other parts of Alaska also tell of great voyages in traditional boats. Oscar Kawagley, in his interview, relates the legend of the five brothers who possibly traveled around the Pacific Rim in skin boats.[8] Moses Paul, birch bark canoe builder, remembers his father-in-law sitting with him at Alki Point in Seattle, telling him there is a time recorded in the stories when boats representing all the Alaska Native people gathered there and some continued on down the coast to California.[9]

The Project
In the Alaska Native Heritage Center project, *Qayaqs and Canoes: Paddling into the Millennium*, only the angyapik from St. Lawrence Island represents a craft that is still actively made and used for hunting in its original form. The Alaska Eskimo Whaling Commission mandates that the whale hunters of St. Lawrence Island use traditional skin-covered boats for the strike. The same is true for the Iñupiat whalers of the north using their umiaks. The other boats in the project are revival examples of ancient arts.

However, many Native elders and others feel there still exists a need and a place in today's world for the old ways of the ancestors. The success of *Qayaqs and Canoes: Paddling into the Millennium* attests to the importance of utilizing traditional ways of knowing to impart significant cultural values, passing them on to future generations. In order to accomplish this transmission of knowledge, an apprentice or apprentices accompanied each master boat builder on his journey of traditional boat construction. In some cases, these students took their newly gained skills back to their homes and are, in turn, teaching others. Also, the project has been well documented by means of a video production, many in-process photographs and this book.

Previous page: Russian Orthodox priest Father Benjamin blesses the boats. Left: Philip Blanchett and John Chase drumming with the Kicaput Singers and Dancers at the dedication ceremony.

In addition to the cultural advantages in looking to tradition, there are practical reasons for using traditional boats that will be made clear in the narratives of the boat builders.

The project highlighted some interesting directions for the future. In the case of a few of the boats, traditional, cultural and gender boundaries were crossed in the quest for re-learning the technology. Males performed skin sewing tasks that were traditionally in the females' domain, and vice versa. In two cases, with a kayak and the dugout, females set precedents by taking on the traditional carving roles of males.

During the five months of the project, there was an aura of urgency, fueled by the desire to learn quickly so the culture would not lose the knowledge again.

Revival

With the renewed interest in traditional Alaska Native culture in the past twenty years, traditional boat building technology is taking its rightful place. Skin boat technology is being taught as part of Native cultural programs in Nanwalek, Kodiak, Kwigillingok and on St. Paul Island, to name a few. These and projects such as *Qayaqs and Canoes: Paddling into the Millennium* in Anchorage, and a few others around the state, focus long-overdue attention on this important activity.

Birch bark canoes have been made recently in Chalkyitsik, Minto, and Fairbanks. There is a resurgence of the technology in Canada and in the bordering states of the U.S. where the bark craft were traditionally used.

New dugout canoes have been carved in Sitka, Wrangell, Hoonah, Glacier Bay, Metlakatla, Ketchikan, Saxman and Haines as well as many locations in British Columbia and Washington State. In 1989, the State of Washington celebrated its centennial. Part of this giant celebration was "Paddle to Seattle," which revitalized the ancient canoe technology among the canoe-making first nations of the West Coast. Canoes were built and paddled into Seattle from the coastal towns of Hoh and LaPush. They were met and joined by a flotilla of others from the Suquamish, Lummi, Tulalip and Heiltsuk nations.[10] This monumental gathering gave birth to future gatherings of traditional canoes that take place at least every three years in various locations in Washington and Canada.

In the spring of 1999, the community of Sitka sponsored their first biennial "Gathering of Canoes" at which they dedicated their newly-carved, thirty-five-foot dugout canoe. Nick Tanape, Alutiiq kayak builder, organizes gatherings of kayaks called "Tamanta Katwhluta" in Homer for the Pratt Museum every two years. These are vessels that truly bring people together.

The canoe is a metaphor for community; in the canoe as in the community, everyone must work together. Paddling or "pulling" as a crew over miles of water requires respect for one another and a commitment to working together, as the old people did. All facets of the contemporary canoe experience — planning, building, fundraising, practicing, traveling — combine to make our communities strong and vital in the old ways. – David Neel[11]

The boats in this project certainly brought people together. Families and extended families were enlisted by the masters to assist. Camaraderie formed among the boat-building community. Eight Alaska Native cultural groups were represented among the boat builders and skin sewers. An atmosphere of generous sharing pervaded throughout the summer. Master builders visited others, bringing tools to share, ones they had discovered worked for a specific task. Skin sewers traded secrets. The intensity among this group was acute as they dedicated themselves to learning the "watertight" stitch. They talked about their grandmothers and what they had passed down to them to use today. Traditional Native foods and materials were brought out and shared along with the old stories and songs. Each boat became a new story in its own right. One skin sewer remarked as she was stitching, "We will be telling our own grandchildren about how we sewed this kayak."

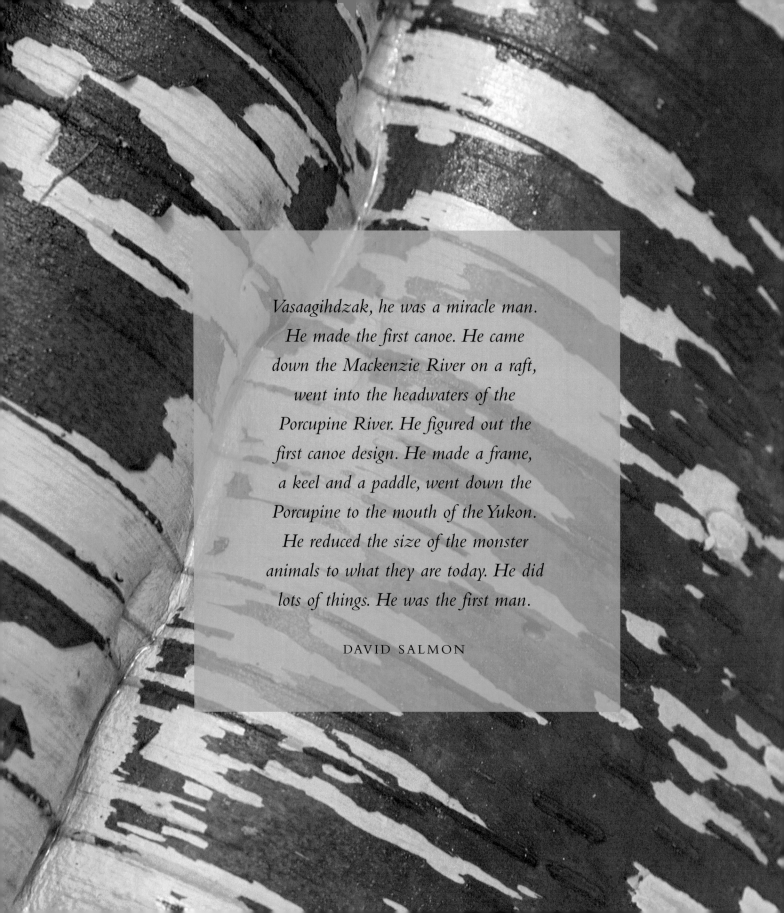

Vasaagihdzak, he was a miracle man.
He made the first canoe. He came
down the Mackenzie River on a raft,
went into the headwaters of the
Porcupine River. He figured out the
first canoe design. He made a frame,
a keel and a paddle, went down the
Porcupine to the mouth of the Yukon.
He reduced the size of the monster
animals to what they are today. He did
lots of things. He was the first man.

DAVID SALMON

Bark Canoes

The bark canoes of Alaska were lightweight, efficient craft used mainly on the river waterways and lakes of the Interior. They were designed for the specific conditions of the location, from glacier-fed, swift rivers to the calm waters of lakes and sloughs.

These craft were built in various sizes, from small one-man hunting canoes to larger cargo-carrying versions. David Salmon refers below to these larger models as being able to carry a family, their goods and their dogs.

Bark canoes were propelled with single-bladed paddles. The paddlers faced forward. A passenger might sit back-to-back with the paddler, thus facing aft. Howard Luke mentions below a typical Athabascan paddle with a ridge down the middle, which prevents the paddle from chattering in the water. For shallow waters, or when traveling against the current, long poles and/or lines pulled by dogs on shore were used.

Sidney Huntington in his book, *Shadows on the Koyukuk*, describes one of these methods of travel:

The art of poling a canoe would also become lost (as the building of birch bark canoes), although it was a wonderful way to travel. Two poles were used each about four foot long and less than three-fourths inch in diameter. While sitting on his legs the canoeist traveled in the shallows, close to the beach, one pole in each hand, by swinging the poles forward then pushing down and back. One could easily travel five miles an hour in this quiet manner. Hunters liked to use poles for they made less noise than paddles. Whenever the canoe reached deep water, the paddles were used.

Huntington also describes how canoes were made:

Native-built birch bark canoes were fairly common along the Koyukuk in 1921, although building them would later become a lost art. An expert could construct a birch bark canoe surprisingly quickly. A dry sandy spot on the river was selected. Posts were driven into the sand in the outline of the canoe frame. Birch ribs were shaped with knife and axe and tied to the post with long tough spruce roots. Then longitudinal strips of clear split spruce were tied to the ribs, making a framework for the birch bark covering. Sheets of birch bark were stripped from living trees as the sap was rising in the spring, and they were cut to fit the frame allowing overlaps for sewing. The bark sheets were then sewn together with spruce root threads, using a bone awl to open the way for insertion. Bow and stern posts were carved. A piece of bark was cut and fitted over the bow and the upper parts of the skin were trimmed and supported by an inner and outer gunwale. The whole length of the gunwales was then corded with long, flexible spruce rootlets.[12]

Because of its light weight, the bark canoe could be carried across portages and easily maneuvered in the water. It was also a craft that could be quickly mended using materials from the woods along one's journey.

The designs of the early bark canoes were highly developed technologically. This is attested to by the fact that the contemporary recreational canoes of today were developed using the same designs with slight modifications. Native Americans knew how to make the materials available to them work in efficient ways to perform a needed function.

In the mid part of the nineteenth century, canvas was adopted for use in place of birch bark for the skin of the boat. The frame design and construction materials remained the same. The canvas was more durable and lasted longer.

Old canoe frames with canvas skins are found in museums and villages today. Very few original birch bark canoes exist as they become quite fragile with age. The bark splits due to climatic conditions and handling. There are, however, old photographs and models that can be accessed for reference.

Athabascan tradition bearer and canoe maker, Howard Luke, lives at his camp on the Tanana River ten miles west of Fairbanks. He builds canoes, dog sleds and fish wheels from local natural materials. He relates memories and his knowledge of the technology

Howard Luke's Recollections
Down at Sixteen Mile (on the Tanana River) there was a man named Old Man Silas and he used to build canoes. He used willows for the ribs and a certain part of a spruce root for the bow. All he used is a crooked knife. He built a lot of canoes, all birch bark.

In the old days, people were very protective about building the canoe. The men were the ones that did the ribs, the side pieces and the bow. Old Man Silas didn't have no wife so he had to do the sewing by himself. The women usually do the sewing because they do such fine work.

I've built a few canoes in my time. I use an awl for sewing the birch bark. The blade has to be flat. The size of it depends upon how thick your roots are. This way you don't split the bark. You use spruce for the side pieces (gunwales), about an inch-and-a-half wide. The bark fits between the two pieces of spruce. Later on, the whole thing will shrink. You can use birch for the ribs but they have to be very thin. We use willows. We don't use a tape measure for measuring. We use our hands, hands-to-our-elbow, like that. That's the way we measure the parts of the canoe, by using our hands, arms, etc.

We gather the materials in the springtime when the sap is running. You have to see how the weather is. Right now the wind is blowing and we had a late spring. The bark doesn't come off. If the tree is in the sun, it will be easier.

When you take bark, you just take some from each tree. You let the tree live. If the tree dies, you use that for wood. We never wasted anything. You roll it inside-out and put it in a cool place. We used to tie the roll with willow bark. We didn't have no string those days.

When you get your spruce roots, if it's the right time of year, the bark should just come right off the root with a knife, should just slip right off. You look for spruce trees with long needles. They'll have the best roots. When you get your wood, you get an axe and you poke it in there and take a piece of wood out. Then you pull on that wood and if it pulls straight, it's a good straight grain.

With the birch and willow, you bend them and if they bend easy and don't break, it's good wood for the ribs. Our people never steamed their birch, like for the ribs, never did. You just have to get it at the right time so it bends easy. Steaming weakens the wood.

I've done it so many times that I can just look at a tree and tell you whether it's good or not. If I'm going to bend it, I don't look for a really white birch. The bark's got to be a little brown. And that's the one that's strong, tough. The white one is kind of brittle.

When you go after that spruce root wood for the bow you just take your axe and just chop alongside and find that root. The trunk of the tree becomes the bottom of the bow and the root is the turn-up. You can't just bend your own for this. This root is very strong. It'll be there forever.

For the pitch, you look around for the brown one. You don't want that yellow; you can get some of that, but mainly you want that brown pitch. And what they used to do to see if it was strong, is chew it. If your gums stick together, that's the kind of pitch you want. It's older pitch. Them days they didn't have no tar or

Women sewing birch bark on a canoe in a traditional crib which helps

align the frame near the village of Moosehide, Canada, circa 1899.

A man paddles his birch bark canoe on the lower Yukon river circa 1825.

Anchorage Museum B7227.60

nothing. That thing's gotta be strong. That's how they test it; they chew it. Then to make it even stronger, they used to put hair in it. I used moose hair. You just dice it up. The men usually do the pitching. They use a stick and put it on the seams.

A rat canoe is a one-man canoe. You sit right in the middle but another man can sit behind. You put your backs against each other. That way, if that canoe is tippy, you can guide it together.

We built a canoe out at Bush Lake and we rat (hunt muskrats) one spring. There were a lot of rats that time. Rats were thirty-five cents apiece and that was a lot of money them days. I didn't know that I was putting all my rats on one side of the canoe. I finally started going and the canoe went right over with me. That taught me a lesson, you know. My mother always tell me that but it goes to show I didn't listen. She said, "You gotta be careful in your ratting canoe. And you never shoot sideways; always shoot straight ahead." Even a little twenty-two has a kick to it. It can knock you off balance and over you go!

We make our paddles with a ridge down the middle of the blade. If your paddle is just flat and you hit a swift current, you're putting all your strength on it and the paddle will just shake. That's what caused people to turn over.

Isaac Jonathan (at left) and two unidentified
men in canoes on the Yukon, circa 1896.

Charles F. Metcalf / Alaska State Library Collection PCA 34-121

You always carry two sticks with you too, so if you get on a sandbar, you use those to get off. We'd carry a can for bailing because if you are along the cut bank and get a hole, you have to bail until you can get ashore to fix it. But usually the canoes didn't leak. People used to take care of their canoes. They'd put them up in the shade to protect them.

Many years ago they didn't have no nails or other stuff so you got get the right kind of material. If you're gonna do it, you got do it right. Get birch with no knots on it. Get good strong roots and wood. It takes a lot of time. You just got to walk and look, or go on the river and see what you can find. It takes time. All trees, everything is alive. And that's what we go by. It's called respect. When I was a kid, my mother used to cut birch bark. And every time she do that, she would pray to that thing, "Come back, come back again." If you respect the material, it will be there for you.

And every time you're working on something like shaving wood, you clean it up. That's respect. 'Cause people walk around that thing. In them days, they were particular about young girls walking around there. You don't leave your tools lying around. Put them away. Take care of them. It pays to have sharp tools. That's how you cut yourself, with dull tools. That's respect. That's *Gaaleeya*, our luck." [13]

Athabascan Birch Bark Canoe, Black River Style

Name: Tryah (Otter, in Gwich'in language)

Length: 12'6"   Width: 27"   Depth: 1'   Weight: 25 lbs. (approx.)
Materials: birch bark covering, spruce wood frame, birch ribs, spruce root lashings, spruce pitch caulking, sealant.

Master boat builder: David Salmon, Chalkyitsik, Alaska
Apprentice: Tom O'Brien

David Salmon is chief of his village, Chalkyitsik, and an Episcopal priest. Tom O'Brien is a former woodsman and an anthropologist who is currently working on his Ph.D. and lectures in anthropology at the University of Alaska, Fairbanks.

Vasaagihdzak, he was a miracle man. He made the first canoe. He came down the Mackenzie River on a raft, went into the headwaters of the Porcupine River. He figured out the first canoe design. He made a frame, a keel and a paddle, went down the Porcupine to the mouth of the Yukon. He reduced the size of the monster animals to what they are today. He did lots of things. He was the first man.
— David Salmon

DAVID SALMON

I was born in Salmon Village, 1912, January 14. That's a long time ago. Eighty-eight years ago. Next year I will be eighty-nine and then on to ninety. I don't know how far I'm gonna go from there. Maybe I'm going take off, I don't know. I'm a slave Indian; I serve my people.

I'd like to talk about the migration, you know, the migration of our ancestors. I know the story of the Indian people when they said they came up the Yukon. I think they came into the Yukon at Anvik. That's where they found the Athabascan bone, the old one. The Indian Story, one little piece of story is:

David Salmon.

It says they go up the Yukon. They go up the Yukon two bends, maybe three bends. Then for a hundred years, another hundred years, nothing happened. They expected this water come from someplace. They don't know. Maybe they run into monster too, a scary monster. They don't know where this water come from. They follow it and then they move up two more bends and they stay there. This took thousands of years to follow the Yukon this way.

I remember about the canoe. When I was a little boy, about seven or eight years old, I sit behind my father in the birch bark canoe and we go up-stream from the village, go up ten miles, look around hunting. We'd come back down in half the time. In that time he used arrow, used arrow for ducks. He got a little .22 anyways, single-shot shotgun. But also he got arrow, all the time. So that's where he started and that's what I remember, what it was like riding in a birch bark canoe.

The first birch bark canoe I saw my father make was 1922. In 1922, I was about ten years old. And I helped my father. I always helped my father to hold a stick here, hold this there. He told me to do this. That's Athabascan way of teaching the children about the canoe you know, and also the snowshoe too, and also the arrow.

When I was a little boy, I watched my father make the canoe like this and I do everything. I hold the stick and I watched where the birch piece go. He teach me the frame, you know the top frame, how big it's gonna be. It must be just right, you know. And also he teach me about the last stick that goes on the canoe. It has to be tied with the roots.

For this birch bark canoe, the frame is a white spruce. I dried it for one year so it won't be crooked. Because otherwise, it's just gonna get crooked you know. You gotta know what kind of wood to use.

When you cut down the tree with axe, you take a chip and if you see the red ring around, is no good. It's only white that's good and it has to be straight too. You test the grain, break it, you know. If it comes off straight then that tree is good. That tree is straight. Sometimes it's crooked grain. You can't use it because it splits. So I watched my father on this and on making canoe, on how you put the bark on and how you tie it together.

This canoe had to be measured by only the body measurements, don't have no other measure. One wrist and one arm is one kind of measure. And then they measure the bottom of the canoe where you sit. This also according to the Indian measure, is your own body measure. My body measure and your body measure is different. Because if you're gonna build a canoe yourself, you have to use your own hand. So they used their own body measure. They measure the birch bark for the canoe like that too.

Tom and I always work together. He and I met when he came up to Chalkyitsik. We went up to Big Meadow; that's where all the people got killed. That was in the early days, before the white people came. I was thinking about it and I told the University that I want to find that place, you know, find a bone or something. I'm gonna put a cross there and re-bury them. I can make a burial service.

Tom came and I showed him around. We went over to dig and we found a fireplace, because in the early days when the people got killed, they just burned each other. In Yukon Flats, they don't bury each other. They just pile the bodies up and burn, burn until all gone, turned into black. We looked for something like that for a sign. We don't find anything anyway but only one place we find a fireplace, but that's not it. So that's why I met him and then later on we work together and finally he want to write my story. He's a carpenter too and he got all the tools we need. He works hard.

He help me write about my tools. My tools, is a long story behind each tool. Each arrow, long story behind it, how they use it, how long they use it and why they use it. All that is in a storybook. And we're gonna put this canoe in the tool book too.

Up the Black River, they used to make canoes. There is some people, they make a big canoe too,

Tom O 'Brien sews bark to bow of birch bark canoe.

Behind, David Salmon shows Karen Refredi how to lash roots.

family canoe. That Black River has lots of birch way up about two hundred miles from Chalkyitsik. The Athabascan always making canoe in a rocky place so they can rub the wood against the big rocks up there. In the early days, before the white people came, they rub the wood against a big stone. All the rock is a file. Pretty soon they make the wood smooth.

There's lots of rock there. That's why they build canoe there. And right across from there, there's lots of birch. That's where they get their birch bark, birch and roots. And then they go over this way and they build a canoe. In one place, they said one time they build over eighty canoes. That's a canoe building place there!

And then they bring those canoes to Fort Yukon because in those days there's no birch growing in the Yukon Flats. A hundred fifty miles across the flats, there's no birch. Down around Chalkyitsik there's just bushy ones. It's hard to find tall ones these days. This one we have here came from Fairbanks, down toward Nenana.

Red ocre was used to color the frame.

In 1930 was the last canoe made by an old man in Chalkyitsik. He make a family canoe. It was about twenty-four feet, big one. They put all their family in it, their things in it, their dogs and go everywhere. Around the gravel bar, where it's shallow, they use stick instead of paddle.

I have a training stick we use to train people. There's two spruce and then they put the bark inside and they tie the bark to the sticks. That's how the Athabascan women learn. When they are a little girl they do this. They have to grow up with it. They learn and then they can sew the canoe. The old women turn it over to the next generation… old Athabascan teaching for thousands of years. Without this they don't know how.

This is what happens when we finish a canoe: they watch the women sewing the roots. Someone yells, "Hey, this is the last tie. Everybody come." It's very important, the last tie they make. They come out of their skin houses and gather around. The last time I made a canoe, there were about thirty, forty people. They circle around and dance, dance, dance. And then we make a speech. We make a speech about the canoe, about the country and how we survived. If it wasn't for the canoe, we not gonna get food and all that. Without this canoe, we're not going to survive. People from the east, north, west and south come and we sing "ha ho." That means good things are going to happen. It's gonna be a lucky canoe. The song is said like that, two Indian words. Then we say "hey, hey." That means God is in His heaven. That's the song I made.

Canoe, it's just about over, so canoe is very important for young people to make. From now on, I think our children are going to learn. I even made a potlatch for the young people to show we respect them. These canoes, this is the way we lived for ten thousand years. I'm proud of my people today. They're doing good.

TOM O'BRIEN

I was born in Bismarck, North Dakota. When I was six, we traveled to Oregon, lived there for about three years and then on to California. I went to high school in southern California and when I graduated, I got an associate degree right off the bat. I was basically sixteen years old when I graduated from high school. So I had an associate degree by eighteen. My parents wanted me to continue but I really wanted to move to the woods.

I came to Alaska with my newly wed wife in 1978 just for the sole purpose of moving out into the woods and with the idea of living there year-round. We lived in the bush for eleven years. I had already lived two years traveling the continental divide in the Rocky Mountains on horseback and traveled probably about five thousand miles, built illegal cabins, and wintered up in the high country. I spent my twenty-first year at about nine thousand feet in this seven-by-ten-foot cabin I built myself and wintered there for five months without seeing anybody.

In 1994, I was working on my BA in anthropology and doing quite a little bit of research about the Fort Yukon area. I trapped and lived in that area for eight years. One of the professors up there had heard that nobody was working with David Salmon so he contacted me. I went out to Chalkyitsik and we did an archaeological survey dig.

David Salmon wraps gunwales together with red-dyed spruce root.

Photo by Mike Conte

That's when I first met David. It was pretty amazing because he was already in his mid-eighties; that was six years ago. He had a rucksack and a heavy shovel and a .30-06. We were going through black spruce burn where they were all laying over to the side. He had to put his leg way up and over. He was just going along fine. We got along real well and we visited and visited about the old times and old stories and stuff.

David wanted to write his life story and so I asked, "Do you want some help?" We have probably about fifty hours of tape and maybe seven hundred pages of transcripts. I have to finish the write-up on that.

In the course of our work together, he built a really beautiful tool collection. I was working with him on that, documenting the tool collection. I also was working on a master's thesis. It got to the point where I could hardly juggle all those things at once, so I asked David, "Can I make this tool project my master's?" He was real happy with it. What I ended up with is a really nice product out of that and a master's that was done. David and I are real pleased with it.

There's a whole bunch of different tools in there: fishing, hunting and general-purpose tools. There are games and the stories associated with all those. I illustrated also, so everything is illustrated to scale, all the major attributes of everything. In other words, if you look at the arrow, you may want to build that arrow in the future. Not only is there the descriptive narrative, but there's the actual artifact that you can just lay it right up next to like a blueprint. You can take a template and take it right off of it.

It's been an on-going process. Scientific illustration takes a long time, and then there's the writing. I work a lot with videotape, because when David is describing something to me, a process, I recontextualize it. I drafted this for an academic audience but there have been several offers to have it published "as is" from various publishing concerns. But we wanted it to be the most thorough book on material culture in the Interior. I probably need about a year and half of continuous work to finish these writing projects.

We've wanted to add the canoe from the get-go. It's really important to have that in there. I'm really excited about the canoe because I always wanted to work on a birch bark canoe. I didn't undertake it before because I knew there were a lot of hidden things about one. David told me "Nothing easy about canoe," and that's true. Every little thing is difficult and painstaking, but it's a real pleasure.

13

These types of craft are suited perfectly for the portion of the world David comes from because they're lightweight and can be portaged easy. They're stable and resilient for a good canoe man. For the average person that is used to a Coleman canoe, they'd probably flip it right away when getting in one of these. But for somebody that knows what he or she is about, like David, they're fine. When he was a boy, he could just get up and stand in one. You'll notice that this one is narrow in the hull and it's flat-bottomed. It doesn't have an over amount of free board.

The Process of Construction
To build a canoe of this type, the selection of your raw materials is more than half the battle. Seasonal, as well as geographical considerations are most important when gathering the spruce, birch, birch bark, spruce root and pitch. The wooden frame pieces are generally roughed out into staves and stringers. The bark is cut from the trees in the spring of the year and rolled up. It takes three rolls of bark for a canoe. The builder works with a hatchet, crooked knife and saw to finish the individual pieces that will comprise the frame.

The next step is to prepare the building site. A working platform of dirt is built up to elevate the project to a suitable height so the workers are not straining their backs. Temporary wooden stakes are cut and used to hold the project in place while under construction. The keel frame is made and placed on the platform. The stem and stern pieces are set at each end of the keel frame. The gunwales come next and then the ribs. A thin plank is lashed on both sides of the craft to add strength to the hull. The entire frame is temporarily held in place with ties until the bark covering is secured. Finally, the entire frame is dyed with red ochre.

The frame is covered with three pieces of birch bark which form the bottom, the port and starboard sides. The bark is sewn together with split spruce root, pulled taut, and sewn to the gunwales with a wrapping of spruce root. Next, the bark is sewn to the stem and stern with rawhide (babiche).[14] A piece of bark is formed to fit the bow section and forms a splash deck. The thwarts are added to the fore, aft and mid sections. Finally, the seams are caulked with boiled spruce pitch to make them watertight.

The bow and stern are made from white spruce. The stern is higher than the bow; that's done intentionally. That's the style for the people where David comes from. The gunwales and interior frame are white spruce. The hull down at the bottom, and the strips that are along the side that are about two-and-a-half inches wide, are white spruce. But all the ribs are birch which bends easier. What David does, is he'll take a piece of a birch about stovepipe size and quarter it. Then he'll knock himself out a rough stave with an ax. Then when he gets it down to where it's about an inch-and-a-half by an inch, he'll take it down with a crooked knife to the dimension needed, about three-quarters of an inch across and maybe about a half an inch wide at the top, sometimes three-eighths inch.

David turns the inside part of the birch bark out to become the outside of the canoe. I think that is because there's less friction and it's prettier.

For pitching the seams, we try to get the pitch to a nice dark brown. We end up with a strip of smeared pitch about an inch-and-a-quarter to an inch-and-a-half wide. It covers the white spruce roots on both sides and then gives it another quarter inch to spare so it seals the holes as well as the seams. I asked David about adding something to the pitch. I know that in Canada they sometimes use fat and sometimes charcoal but David said that they generally, if anything, put a little bit of lard or fat in.

In the research that I have done with regard to the Interior, many times the canoes were described to be "loaded down to the gunwales." People that were using these all the time would probably bring them right up to the spruce root on the gunwales sometimes, depending on what they were carrying.

To make the material pliable, rolls of birch bark soak in
Lake Tiulana at the Alaska Native Heritage Center.

The framework down at the bottom keeps the majority of everything off the bottom. They have a bilge down there about three-quarters of an inch. A lot of times with the eastern canoes, they have rounded bottoms, more or less, and solid ribs planked on the side and then birch bark. They generally will throw down a bunch of different little wood, runs of sticks, to keep the burden off the bottom.

The color on the dyed roots is just a matter of beauty, I think. I think the design element is a matter of personal preference, just to make it pretty. The amount of wrapping on the gunwales differs from place to place. The Black River style does not cover the entire gunwale. It alternates wrapped with unwrapped sections.

It should be mentioned too that David feels the whole project couldn't be done without the contribution of the split spruce roots. That's an extremely important contribution to the project. Lina Demoski of Anvik made those for this canoe. She had to carefully dig up the roots from living trees and then peel and split them. It is not an easy job.

The Working Relationship

It's always really a pleasure to work with David because he never never loses his temper and screams or yells. He doesn't get too upset about anything. He just goes about his business and when there's something pertinent, he'll say, "Tom, look at this now. This is the way you got to do it." If it's a prescribed rule, he'll tell me, "You can't break this rule." If it's something you can just do for style or something that you can fool around with, then he'll tell me that too. So in other words, he's not just showing me, he's telling me the history of things while we're working.

He teaches by talking and by demonstrating. He'll tell you that he can't teach unless he has something in his hand. That's the old way that it was always done, and it's the best way to teach. It's showing people what to do, giving them the chance to do it and to perfect the technique and to pass it on to the next generation.

The Future

I'd love to make a canoe in the near future with my fifteen-year-old son when I have this fresh in my mind. It needs to be continued. Also, I'll work toward trying to get the academics to really recognize that this stuff has to be supported, the knowledge has to be transmitted and that's not always easy to do. When people are in academic departments or whatever they might not understand that if a generation lapses without that, that's it. You can forget the whole thing in a generation.

This Project

A highlight of this project, I think, is probably the spirit of the whole thing. We're caught between a rock and a hard place in that we have deadlines and different things that both of us are involved in. We're far from home, but at the same time, the idea of doing a good job and taking your time and wanting to produce a good solid thing that's decent and holds tradition is there all the time.

There's a good-natured aspect to things: sharing and visiting, and mentorship, that I think is much different. Then there is singing, joking, praying, asking for strength, guidance and help to produce a good thing and not let people down. That's a very, very traditional cultural thing here: to do a good job so that we don't let the people down. So, the first thing we do in the morning when we eat our breakfast, is pray.

I feel extremely fortunate, always have, to be able to work with David. It just doesn't happen all the time to people. I've been extremely excited about this project ever since I heard about it. I'm just tickled pink to be involved with it and honored.

Canoe frame members are tied together with nylon sinew.

Athabascan Birch Bark Canoe

Name: Chada's Baqee, Grandfather's Canoe

Length: 7'   Width: 27"   Depth: 1'   Weight: 20 lbs.
Materials: Birch bark covering, spruce wood frame, spruce root and babiche lashings, spruce pitch sealant

Master boatbuilder: Moses Paul, Nenana, Alaska
Apprentices: Russell Silas, Demeris Hudson, Christopher Crookham
Root gatherers: Debbie and Cindy Charlie

We had interesting and informative trips into the woods outside of Nenana to gather spruce wood and roots with Moses. The day was typical of summer in the Interior, hot and dry. We drove along logging roads until Moses found promising trees. He then showed us how a special part of the trunk and root, at the base where it enters the ground, becomes the part used for the bow and stern of the canoe. One has to look for just the right natural curve of the root below ground, extending up into the trunk of the tree.

Later that day, mosquitoes swarmed in the seventy-seven-degree weather as Debbie Charlie and her sister Cindy joined us deep in the woods to gather spruce roots for sewing the bark on to the canoe. We entered a black spruce grove on a hill. The forest floor of moss was very dry.

Debbie and Cindy went to work, walking through the woods looking for tall, straight trees that were growing without other trees close by. When they found a likely tree, they went to work with garden trowels. Moss, dirt and mosquitoes flew into the air as the women pulled back the ground exposing long runner roots. It was not an easy job and required patience and know-how. As they worked, they talked about their grandmother who used to make these root-gathering trips with them. It was apparent they had learned their lessons well from this tradition bearer as they adeptly gathered the offerings of the forest.

Moses Paul holds spruce roots that will be used for lashings.

They looked for roots that ran ten to fifteen feet in length, the longer the better. They followed the root as far as they could and then carefully pulled it out of the ground. These were put into plastic bags to hold what little moisture there was. It was hard to find good roots because everything was so dry, unseasonably so for June. Later the sisters peeled the bark and split the roots into three parts. These were then coiled and put away until they were needed for sewing.

When it came time to sew the bark onto the canoe, Moses told us that his grandmother would have done that part. "The women were the experts at this, much better that I am." But, he and Russell dove into the task along with the help of a few women that came to their assistance. Demeris Hudson, the interpreter for the Athabascan site at the Heritage Center, was enlisted and surprised herself by teaching herself how to split the additional roots that were needed. Everyone on the project was there to learn as each picked up ancestral skills that had almost been forgotten.

MOSES PAUL

I was born in Nenana area, September 5, 1933. And I'm from Nenana, Old Minto, Kantishna, Coby Hill, a place they call Canyon on the Alaska Range. The Wood River area was the main area we go back and forth to each spring and winter.

Most of my education came from my grandmother. She was my main source of learning and knows all the necessities of preserving our way of living and how to build things. She showed me how to work on canoes and canoe paddles, snowshoes, and some parts of the lacing on the dog sled, making dog horns and home items. She was my main source of getting Native-way of training.

Her name was Agnes Thomas. Actually I don't really know where she came from. The only place that we have heard that she came from was from the Tyonek area. I remember when I was very young, she had

mentioned big waves and that's one place that I know has big waves, so that must've been the truth that she's from that area.

I built a canvas canoe with my grandmother. It was far back, probably around 1940, '41. She did everything, the frame, the sewing. That's how I got my education; she did it all. In fact, the only thing my grandfather did was he went out and carried back the material. She did all the carving. The kids were the only ones that helped her. She talk Athabascan and the only time she did that was to get something and that was it. If she told story, I couldn't understand her.

My grandmother mentioned they use canoes, but in the late-1800s they started using canvas to cover them. They never did switch back to birch bark. They used the same frame but all canvas. The pattern is the same all over Alaska, except there are some the front end and the rear end is a little different. Other than that, the design is all the same.

My dad mentioned that one time there was about seven hundred canoes gathered in Nenana. I guess they went down to Tanana, into the Yukon. I guess there was some kind of battle going on down that way. There was supposed to have been some research done on that but I never heard any more.

There were some canoes that used willows, real small. They used that for spring fish camp and for hunting, a one-man canoe. The one my grandmother and I used when I was a youngster, the bottom part was very thin. The bottom was from spruce. The tree was cut down and was split in several pieces. It was cut down to maybe eighteen feet long and they used that for the bottom part there and up to the gunwales. I think there's a space about four or five inches where the canvas fits on.

The other one, I guess, is just that one-man canoe that maybe about eight pieces goes on there. That's the kind they would go out ratting in. Actually, I never have counted, but they come back with at least thirty, forty muskrats. What they do for reinforcing the canoe

Moses works on frame of hand-split

white spruce for his birch bark canoe.

Moses heads up the Tanana River with Howard Luke to look for bark.

Howard's dog Schatzie accompanies Moses in the bow of the boat.

Previous page: Birch trees overhang the cut bank on the Tanana River.

material, they said they put in very thin willows, leaves and all. They just put them on the bottom of the canoe. That's so that it doesn't break. So, about up to forty muskrats I guess they could hold. They do that also when they kill moose. They just go out and get brush. We just get all the smallest willows we can find and lay them in there so the weight does not break the ribs. When hauling meat, it can take quite a bit of weight that way.

We always used a single paddle. We never used a double paddle that I can remember. Some canoes are pretty tippy, but the bigger ones we had, they were pretty stable. The one-man canoes are the ones that are tippy. They were about ten, twelve feet long. The two-man canoes would run up to twenty feet I guess. They'd haul quite a bit of camping gear in them.

For going up-river they used to give us a long rope, then they'd hitch up three or four dogs and pull the canoe along the sand bar. They'd have a long pole and hold the big canoe out in the open water. I used to run along the sand bar with the dogs and keep them going. They don't do that anymore either.

The canoe we put together here at the Alaska Native Heritage Center is all spruce. For the bow and stern we used the part of the spruce root that curves from the ground up. We used the real small spruce tree for the ribs, young spruce, about an inch thick. We split them. Nowadays they use nails to hold them together. This one is of natural materials: spruce gum, spruce roots, rawhide or babiche, and young trees that are spliced together and birch bark. We used all spruce because

Debbie and Cindy Charlie harvest birch bark.

once it dries out, it's real lightweight. One man can carry a canoe by himself.

It was really dry when we went into the woods to pull our roots. It was just one of those types of years that was very odd and everything was just so dry, it made things real difficult. By this time of year, the sap should've been running about month ago, but it didn't happen. I don't really know why, it was just simply dry. We almost had to force the bark off there because it was so dry. When we look for the birch bark, the smoother, the better. But we just didn't run into that this year.

We traveled over some three hundred miles to get the material we needed for the canoe. Another reason we were having so much trouble to find it was that we run into people's signs that say "No Trespassing" and that would force us out. We run into places where they got farms where we didn't even know they had farms. We had to move on.

When were are gathering the pitch, we look for the lightest part we could find. Again, where we go, we just couldn't find it. The ones we found was rock solid and that's where we come in with the idea of boiling it, softening it up and separate the pieces of wood that's in there. I had to mix it with marine polyethylene. I thought we got enough here. I couldn't count on it, so I just used the man-made glue.

We were never taught how to take care of the canoe after it was made. I always asked that question. I don't know whether you could keep that thing moist by spraying it or keeping a wet sheet over it. I don't think

25

it should be too much trouble because it's moister air down here (Anchorage) than up north. Up north is a lot drier. So I never was taught how to, but I remember the earlier days when I was very small is when they got ready to use the canvas canoe. They just stick it in the water, dip it a couple of times and took it out and let it dry. I think that moistened up the ribs and it don't dry up.

I don't know how long the bark would last before it had to be replaced. The only danger, the only thing you'd have working against you, is the air itself.

The thing we used to do when were out hunting is just carry a tin can with us and if the canoe needed patching, you just stop anywhere, build a fire, melt down the pitch and patch it up there and go. That's one good thing about pitch. You can put it on and you don't have to worry about it having to dry. The water will cool it off real quick and it gets hard.

The tools we got today are more modern. In our time, the only thing we had was small hatchet and the knife they call crooked knife. That was used for cutting curves in making canoe paddle. That was the main purpose of having that crooked knife. It put the curve in the paddle. They had a tool that they used to have like an edger. They don't have them anymore. The only time I've seen that, one gentleman I think from Minto, he was the last person I saw have old tools. So in our area there's none left.

There is one type preservative for the wood that's kind of orange, reddish-orange color. They get that off the Alaska Range somewhere. They grind it up from rocks and make it into powder form that they rub onto the canoe paddle and all. That material goes onto the canoe and preserves it. That's very scarce. I ask about it and nobody seem to know where to get it. My

Cindy Charlie pulls birch roots that will be used for canoe lashings.

grandmother never did say where she got hers. I know it came from the Alaska Range, from the Wood River.

My grandma used rocks for sandpaper. There's some way that you can use sand and the ashes from campfire for cleaning compound. That campfire ashes, there's something in there that really cuts. If you have pitch on your hand and you lather it up, it comes off.

This is the first time I have worked with Russell (Silas). I called him and talked to him on the phone and asked him if he was willing to come down and he said, "Yes." He's familiar with Native crafts.

I taught him about the trunk of the tree that we use for the bow and I taught him about the pitch. Then I taught him about four items we use that are the main source of material if he is to do it the traditional way, without using nails and screws and whatnot. He knows how to gather these materials now.

This program we're in, I'd like to see them expand it. This is the first time ever anybody approached us. How we find out is through a newsletter and we submitted a proposal for it. For a while we didn't think anybody noticed our proposal until we got a phone call. I think this kind of program is needed all over.

RUSSELL SILAS

I'm nineteen years old. I was born in Fairbanks Memorial Hospital and I grew up there until I was five years old. My parents are Elaine Silas and Freddie Paul. I moved to Nenana, stayed with my father there for about a year and a half, went to school there. I also went back and forth from Minto to Nenana. I stayed in Minto for awhile and then go stay with my father in Nenana.

People from Nenana and Minto, there's some relationships there. My grandmother and grandfather, they were related from down that way somewhere. I don't know, it's just real close to Old Minto. Same language.

When I was a little kid in Minto I used to like to dance and everybody just gets down and dances. So I learned how to Indian dance.

The elders in Minto trained me. They pushed us very hard, you know. Sometimes they come by school to do some Native language. Also they come by and show us how the birch bark baskets are made. But mostly, they'd come in and tell some stories about what's going on, like back in their days. They tell us some stories. Some of those elders are Evelyn Alexander, my grandma Sarah Silas, there's Rosco Charlie and his wife. Another is Susie Charlie, Jonathan David, and there's Neil Charlie and Geraldine. Jonathan David came to school to teach us how to build a drum.

I've never seen one of these bark canoes being built. I've seen my uncle Jonathan make a canvas one down in Minto back when I was growing up. I don't think he completed it. It's like half done. He had the frame with the canvas around it. I didn't get to see him finish it. It looked pretty nice.

I'm learning about the long poles we use for the canoe, like when you cut them down they're supposed to be straight, no curving. Has to be just a straight tree. And the bow and the bottom of the boat, we're working on that part. I'm loving this. It's a good thing to know how to build stuff.

The most often asked question by visitors this summer was "What are you making?" I told them how we make the bow. They'd ask questions about the pitch and the roots and the bark. They'd ask where we get it from. I just tell them, "Interior Alaska. My uncle Mo got it. It's in the forest, you know." They ask if maybe there's a way they could get some.

Some other questions were like, "Is this a father-and-son thing?" They were talking about me and uncle Mo.

This one girl, she asked me, "Does it feel good to learn this?" I said, "Yea." Just questions like that.

This is the first time I've made a birch bark canoe. I wanted to do this because I wanted something new, something near my culture and it's pretty fun. I wouldn't mind teaching some other people to build one of these. Maybe I'll make a canoe when I get back to Minto, maybe get a little help from Jonathan David. That would be nice. The old people would love that. Then maybe I can try teaching my friends.

DEBBIE CHARLIE

My grandmother, Mabel Charlie, raised me. She would go out to the woods with me and my sister Cindy and we would pick roots and birch for her birch bark baskets. During the summertime, that's when she did it in Old Minto. She would also make baby baskets with the beads in the back. They used to put moss inside of it to cushion the baby. Then she told us how they used to dye the roots a long time ago was by using berries.

When we'd go out to get the roots, she told me to go to an open area where it's not crowded. The spruce tree would have to be a big, straight one because if the tree is not straight, the roots would be crooked. You don't want crooked roots because you can't split them and they are hard to sew with.

When you find the birch, you want some that doesn't have knots in it. It's the same for the baskets and the canoes. If the bark has knots, it's really hard to pull the bark away from the tree and there are holes in the bark. You take the bark in the spring, when the sap begins to run.

My grandma had this special way of teaching me. If I didn't do it right, I had to tear it out and start over. All that work, and then you had to tear it apart! She pretty much taught me all the traditional values. We even tanned a moose skin together when I was only nine and my sister was eight. I'm interested in teaching these things, keeping the traditional culture and values going.

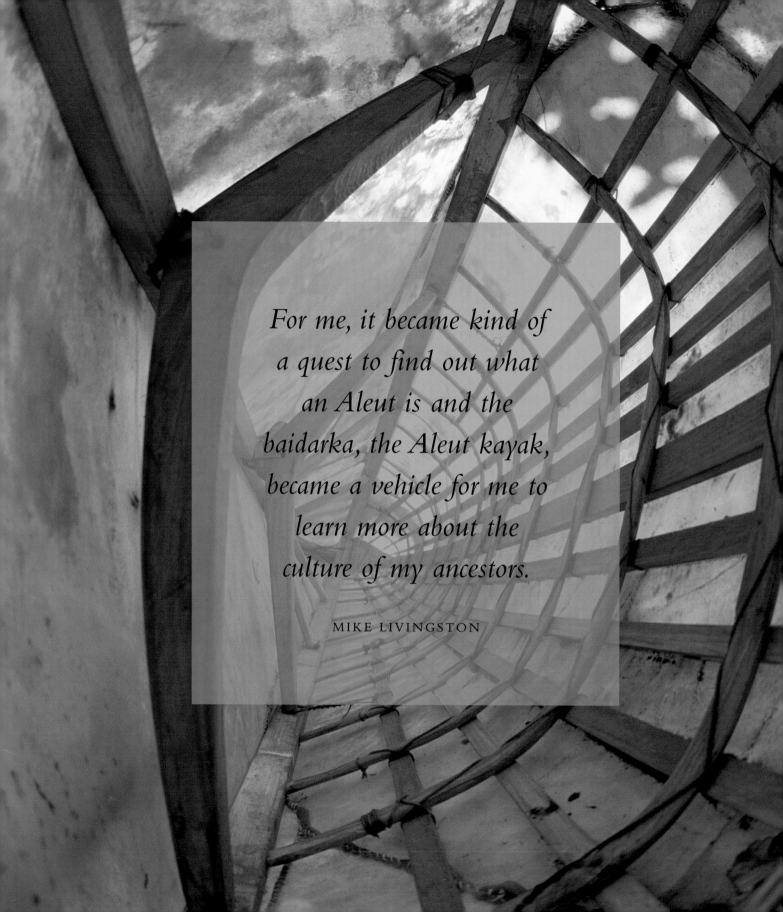

For me, it became kind of a quest to find out what an Aleut is and the baidarka, the Aleut kayak, became a vehicle for me to learn more about the culture of my ancestors.

MIKE LIVINGSTON

Kayaks

A kayak is made of driftwood from the beach for the frame. It is covered with the skin of a mammal, which is sewn with sinew from another animal. A hunter dons clothing made from the intestines of a seal, perhaps a hat of bent driftwood adorned with sea lion whiskers, feathers, beads and ivory from a walrus. He then slips into his kayak, attaches his gut parka to the rim of the hatch and becomes one with the boat, the water and the animals of the sea.

It is a different world when you're sitting in a kayak. You're almost literally sitting in the water. Your rear is below sea level and your hands are constantly touching the sea ocean and the water is undulating beneath of you. It's an awesome feeling. You can get right up to sea life.

On St. Paul in the Pribilof Islands I had the privilege of paddling some baidarkas that the Aleut High School students made. We paddled out to the seal rookeries. It was late at night, probably after midnight, but the sun was still out. The ocean was blue, and the water was shallow to where, even though it might have been twenty to thirty feet deep, you could see the bottom, the big boulders underneath. The fur seals came right out to us. One fur seal stuck its head out of the water. Its skin was kind of blackish when it first came out of the water. Right by the bow of my kayak, he opened up his mouth and I could see his red gums and white teeth. He put his mouth gently on the bow of the baidarka, and he touched his teeth to it. I wasn't really scared because I knew he wasn't trying to bite my kayak, he was just really curious.

– Mike Livingston

History and technology

The Iñupiat, Yup'ik, Alutiiq and Aleut people all used kayaks, decked-over skin boats. Archeological evidence indicates a two-thousand-year history in their use and inferential evidence adds another two thousand years, according to Zimmerly. [15]

These craft were made mainly in regions of treeless terrain from locally available materials. They had to be lightweight enough so one man could handle the boat on shore and in the water. They had to be sturdy and fexible to withstand stormy seas and floating ice. They also had to be highly maneuverable for hunting large sea mammals. The hunter had to be able to approach the animal quietly and then quickly move his kayak into the required positions as the hunt progressed.

Ancient skin boat technology employed remarkable adaptations to accomplish these requirements. To reduce the weight of the boat, a lightweight, yet strong, skin was used as a structural member. This was combined with a skeleton frame composed of thwarts, stringers, ribs, a keelson and gunwales, all lashed together to become a structurally sound, yet flexible, unit. Friction joints of carved bone or ivory were added to the wood at points where a member rubs against or moves across another member. This, combined with a skin that was not rigid, allowed every part of the kayak to move and adjust in maritime conditions.

Kayaks were built mainly with one and two hatches, however a three-hatch configuration was a later innovation that came with Russian contact. The hatch in the middle allowed passengers, such as Russian explorers and missionaries, to be transported by two paddlers.

Both double- and single-bladed paddles were used. A single-bladed paddle was usually taken along and strapped to the deck as a spare.

The accentuated bifid or bifurcated (split) bows of the Alutiiq (Sugpiaq) kayaks have been explained in numerous ways. Nick Tanape, master builder of the Alutiiq boat, is of the opinion that they use that shape for very practical purposes.[16] The flared top portion provides flotation and the bottom portion serves as a cutwater. This configuration provides maneuverability in the rough seas surrounding Kodiak Island, Prince William Sound and the Alaska Peninsula.

Other explanations have ventured into symbolic references such as the bow imitating the form of sea mammals, making the approach of a craft less intrusive. An example would be, as seen when looking at the on-coming bow of the kayak, a sea otter floating on its back. Whatever the reason, these bow forms give unique signatures to these craft.

A kayak was outfitted to carry many hunting implements efficiently. There were thongs for fastening weapons and paddles to the deck; holds for floater boards which carried lines; holds for inflatable skin floats and guards to prevent lances, spears and harpoons from rolling off the deck. They carried siphoning bailers made of wood which were used by a man sucking up water from the bilge into the tube, covering the bottom hole of the bailer with his hand, then releasing the water overboard.

Measurements

A kayak was a man's most prized personal possession. It was built specifically for him, using his body measurements. No system of European measure was employed. For example, a typical measurement would be from an outstretched elbow of one arm to the finger tips of the other arm extending in the opposite direction. Arms outstretched usually represented a fathom (six feet). The height and weight of the individual for whom the kayak was being made were taken into consideration in the design calculations.

Spiritual Connection

Due to the kayak's supreme importance in subsistence activities, the craft took on a spiritual significance in the hunt. Amulets and markings were attached or painted onto the frame and deck. In the Bering Sea and Kuskokwim regions, the cockpit might carry carved representations of a male smiling face and female frowning face, balancing symbols on either side of the paddler which seek protection for him. The horizontal hand grip at the end of each paddle was also incised with a semi-human face, one with a down-turned mouth, the other, up-turned. One represented a woman; the other, a man.[17] Other amulets might be hidden in secret places on the boat to solicit safety for the hunter and ensure a good hunt. These symbols extended to the bentwood hunting hats worn by the paddler. Not only were these hats meant to protect against glare from the water and camouflage the hunter, but added icons, such as the spirals and volutes, were put there to establish a spiritual connection with the powers of the universe.[18]

Each man had, in addition, his own personal markings that he would add to the frame or put inside the deck or on the paddles. These were used for identification. An example of personal deck designs is illustrated on the Kwigillingok boat in this project. That particular eagle design has been passed down for generations through Andrew family lines.

ANGAYUQAQ OSCAR KAWAGLEY

Angayuqaq Oscar Kawagley, Yup'ik indigenous educator, was raised by his grandmother in Bethel. He is presently on staff at the University of Alaska, Fairbanks. Pivotal to his work is the concept of researching and utilizing the best of traditional and western technologies. This interest led him to a doctoral dissertation based upon fish camp technology. He continues to explore the possibilities.

I remember my family and I were always going to fish camp when I was growing up. Our fish camp was

Early seal hunter from Nome, Alaska, with skin-covered

kayak, snowshoes, a sealskin float and a spear.

Anchorage Museum B70-28

Men in kayaks from St. Michael, Alaska.

Anchorage Museum B91.35-4

in what we call Steamboat Slough. I remember the Nunivagmiut, the people from Mekoryuk, Nunivak Island, being there. Many years ago they had what we called the Columbia boats, the Columbia packer boats they used for fishing. Those were special boats; they were sailboats. I remember them coming in with their sailboats and always on the side would be a kayak. That's what they would get into to go ashore to our fish camp. We would purchase sealskins of seal oil from Nunivak or trade dry fish for the seal oil.

I remember getting into one of those kayaks and I almost tipped over. I was told by them that you take your paddle and put in on the outside, the water side, and then you can get in safely. Your kayak is sideways to the beach. So that was my first experience. I was quite small so the hole was really big for me but I did paddle around a little.

Five Brothers

We have many stories in our oral tradition. One is about the five brothers adrift. They were caught in icebergs in the Bering Sea. They apparently floated out into the Pacific Ocean and they may have traveled around the Pacific Rim. They stopped on an island and, what I surmise is, they encountered some monkeys. Another island had some strange people. They didn't communicate the way you and I do; in fact they had no mouths. The story goes that they would smell their food rather than consuming it. But one of the brothers got curious and he felt around and it felt like they had teeth under there. One of them was brave enough for him to make a slit, and sure enough he had a mouth. From then on, after the little membrane was removed from over their mouths, they were able to eat their food. They had many other adventures and it just sounds like to me they went around the Pacific Rim. You can tell from that how seaworthy those kayak are.

Canoes

These five brothers were from the Coast. We are from the Interior so we used canoes more than kayaks. The canoes I remembered were fabric-covered, canvas. The old ones were probably covered in some kind of skin, maybe sealskin. They are thin and light enough. They weren't made of birch bark.

Our people would often get caught in storms. Back in those days, they had seal-gut rain coats that you can tighten around your wrists, around your face and they were large enough to where you could tie your raincoat to the rim of the kayak and no water gets in there. The thing that they had to remember, with the big waves when they started to break, was to go with it and paddle, paddle, paddle. 'Cause if you didn't, then you would roll with the breaking wave. That was one thing my grandmother told me. You keep paddling when you were in those waves, and into them, not sideways.

For the kayaks, they used both double and single paddles. The double paddle, what we call *pangercutik,* was for when you wanted to go as fast as you could. They had thongs right in the front of the kayak where you could slip the paddles when you were not using them. That was also for harpoons, bows and arrows, and then they were right in front of you on the deck. And always the front was a little bit longer than the rear. Very often, when they got seals, they would put the seal inside, back of the paddler.

For the covering, they'd use the bigger seals, the bearded seal, especially on the underside of the kayak. They have stronger skin. The top could be the lighter, made of smaller types of seals. The women and some of the men would sew the skins on wet. When they dried, they would become really compact all around it. For thread, they used sinew from the back of caribou or moose, large mammals.

From my area, the way to waterproof the skin was to take sphagnum moss and mix it up with seal oil and let it become rancid. Then they applied that onto the kayak. I don't know exactly what the moss does. I

33

Sea otter fleet in the Unga area of the Aleutians.

know that it contains some acid. I don't know if the acidity has anything to do with it or not. They would need to repeat that process to keep it waterproof. The skins lasted a long time because they took really good care of them. You probably have seen the crossed poles where they would put their kayaks upside-down, off the ground, so mice and others would not chew on the skin. They took really good care of them, a matter of survival.

The kayaks were made to fit the individual, his stature, his strength. Everything was pretty much made for the individual, like the parkas, and so their bows, to fit the strength and height of the individual.

"The hole on a kayak was a little larger than the individual. When they were moving around as a family, they would have the kids go inside down under the deck and the wife would sit back to back with her husband.

In some instances when they were on the move and a person dies, they would put them inside the kayak, put it out on the tundra and turn it upside-down. Because that was the quickest way to inter the deceased. That was only when they were out hunting. Our normal way was to put them into a fetal position in the qasegiq.[19] They were never to be taken out through the doorway because the *qasegiq* was thought of as being like the reproductive system of the female. It gives life, so a dead person was not to be removed that way, but rather through the skylight. Sometimes their kayak would be put with them at death, but often it was passed on to the son because they were priceless. But I have seen photos the Moravian Church has that show a person's kayak with the grave.

And for the frame they would use certain parts of the wood. The tree trunk, where it becomes a root, is really strong. They would use that for the bow and stern. All the ribbing was tied together with rawhide, sealskin. So when they get damp, it gives a lot of flexibility to the kayak. From what the Danish have written about it, the tensile strength of that is much more than rigid aluminum. You hit the ice with that and the skin will give, whereas the aluminum won't; it is more likely to get punctured. The flexibility was really important for the kayak. The engineering technology was really something.

They had little amulets that would be in the bow. No one would see them. They also might have one on the inner edge of the hole. *Iinrug* is what we call it, our word now for medicine. It was for safety, for protection, and to have the animals give themselves to you.

I caught some of the kayaks, especially when I went to Hooper Bay and I saw some people pulling their kayaks on sleds. They made special little sleds for their kayaks. They always carried these sleds on the back deck of the kayak when they went out hunting for seal. They dragged the kayak on the sled until they got to the water, and then they put it on the back of the kayak. I used to see them go out hunting. I was too scared to go out on the ice. That's not something I grew up with, so although I was invited, I didn't go.

In northern Quebec among the Inuit there, they are going back to using their kayaks. Hopefully it will take on again in our own region because with the fuel prices going up and other things getting to cost a lot more, we may need to go back to it like them. Some of the villages are going back to dog teams.

I think the paddlers were pretty skilled in righting their boats when they turned over. I've found that way up north, the Greenlandic Inuit probably have the best design. They are much shallower. I saw a sixty-eight-year-old demonstrate on a lake in Nuuk, Greenland. He was sixty-eight years old and he flipped over and came right back up. The last time he did it, he stayed under for a while and we all started to panic. But eventually he popped right back up.

Innovation
John Pingayak and I are going to have four or five high school kids work with us to build a kayak but it has to accommodate a small, solar-powered engine and, of course, a battery. We're going to use canvas and a driftwood frame. The battery will run a small electrical motor and turn a shaft. If it works, I am anxious to hear from the elders, their comments. This has been a dream of mine for a long time to use the architecture and the engineering of the kayak, but also meld a sustainable energy source to western technology, so we are not using an internal combustion engine which requires fuel. That's one of the things I have always thought about. And hopefully we will be able to make a semi-subterranean house at some point which again marries our traditional technology with modern materials.[20]

Central Yup'ik Qayaq–Caninermiut Style

Length: 16'8"   Width: 28"   Depth: 18"   Weight: 65 to 70 lbs. (approx.)
Materials: White spruce driftwood, yellow cedar, bearded seal skin covering,
braided nylon lashing for frame, spun cotton and nylon thread for sewing skins,
caulked with grass and sealed with moss and seal oil.

Master boat builder: Frank Andrew Sr., Kwigillingok, Alaska
Master apprentice: Bill Wilkinson
Apprentices: Noah Andrew Sr., Noah Andrew Jr.
Skin sewers: Nellie Andrew, Mary Ann Wilkinson, Catherine Paul,
Margaret Beaver, Andrea Beaver, Lucy Anaver

With the renewed interest in Native boat building this project has brought to light, many of the boat-building enthusiasts are talking about where the next project is going to be and how the time, funding and materials may be found. The Andrew and Wilkinson families in Kwigillingok have already answered this question by forming a non-profit kayak building and research project entitled *Qayanek*. They have constructed a boat-building shed and are involved in creating kayaks based on research conducted with elder Frank Andrew. The other boat builders who participated in this project were impressed by the existence of this organization and also by the dedicated effort of this large and extended family as they set about constructing their kayak. Father and grandfather were teaching sons and grandsons. The grandmother was teaching her large group of sewers the secrets of preparing and sewing with sinew. It was an impressive effort and certainly spoke about the traditional manner in which education took place in Alaskan villages in times past.

The *Qayanek* group assembled their frame in the village, took it apart and brought it to the Anchorage site, and reassembled it for the project. Journal entries written by Bill Wilkinson concerning collecting wood for the kayak in an area of Alaska that is treeless, tell a story that must be similar to stories told by many kayak

Frank Andrew's grandson, Troy Wilkinson, tests his
paddling skills on a lake near his home in Kwigillingok.

makers of the past. It gives us an insight into how laborious and, today, expensive the task of gathering materials can be.

June 5 – Spent the day looking through the village steam bath piles of wood for the curved pieces for the five deck beams…. Much time was spent with a chain saw cutting up stumps to no avail…. Rotten wood was sometimes found or a slight crack. If neither were present, then the grained twisted in undesired ways.

June 6 – Noah went out for wood collection on the Kuskokwim. Tides were not ideal and only a few small stumps were collected…. The region is so barren, no trees grow within a hundred miles. Ninety miles to the north there are some small scrub willows that have no use in a coastal qayaq.

June 7 – Spent the day cutting up what stumps we have to rough-out cross members. After working with a few rough roots, two were acceptable. Because we are working with drift-

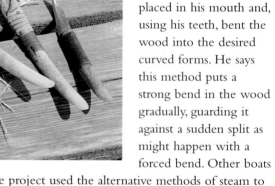

wood, some of the pieces do not always turn out when we remove external wood and get down to final size.

June 15 – A nearby coastal search was conducted while some subsistence activities were being conducted. No acceptable wood was found due to the vast tidal mud flats allowing no access.

June 20 – The effort continued through another individual's woodpile to acquire a suitable driftwood selection for the aft keel piece. Once again the selections were all cut off too short (for steam bath wood) and hours of chainsawing produced only a few low-grade driftwood choices.

July 10 – …Unfortunately the day trip to Tuntutuliak was only successful in searching the west side and could

not cross the Kuskokwim because of the large waves that had arisen because of the winds that came up with the high tide. The expense of this type of authentic construction based on driftwood collection would seem low, however driftwood selection in a treeless region can be very expensive. A number of times a twenty-two-foot skiff would be loaded with a hundred thirty dollars worth of gas and the search yielded few or no useable pieces. Some years, the wood collection is excellent. Not this year!

A unique aspect of the preparation of material for this particular boat was the method used to bend the ribs. Bill Wilkinson demonstrated with pieces of white spruce which he carefully placed in his mouth and, using his teeth, bent the wood into the desired curved forms. He says this method puts a strong bend in the wood gradually, guarding it against a sudden split as might happen with a forced bend. Other boats in the project used the alternative methods of steam to bend their wood or simply soaked the pieces well and then bent them around frames.

FRANK ANDREW
Translated from Yup'ik by daughter Mary Ann Wilkinson

My father's Yup'ik name is Missaq. He's eighty-three. He was born in the year 1917. We use that for his birth date.

At the age of fourteen or fifteen my father got his own first kayak. His father started working on his first kayak during the wintertime, and the following spring he used it to hunt. Two summers after that, on the fourth summer, his father made him a larger kayak. He

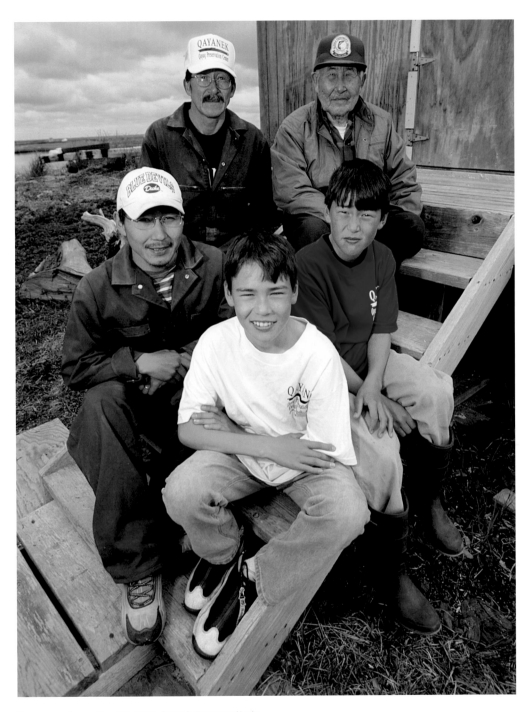

Three generations of kayak builders, Frank Andrew, son Noah
and grandsons Noah Jr., Troy and Ethan. Left: Hand adz and
three curved blade knives, one made by Frank Andrew, one
by his father, and one by his grandfather.

estimates that the year 1958 was the year that they started choosing western boats in our region.

He mentions that traditionally the kayak was the most important possession that they had because they used it to subsist on the land and the ocean. It's the most important one. So since this is the most important material thing that they had, they watched it carefully. They made sure the kayak was in good condition year-round.

After four or five years, not more than five years, they changed the whole covering even though it still looked good. They looked at the frame and if they think one part of the frame is going to break, they replaced it. When they travel, they took extra wooden parts of the kayak and if it needs to be replaced, they replace them.

They learned how to choose the wood from the elders. The elders taught them which part of the tree is good for the certain part of the kayak. It's not just any wood.

The use of the red rock (red ochre) has been passed on from their ancestors. It preserves the wood on the kayak so it doesn't rot. He says with that it doesn't get moldy or get rotten. It helps the wood from breaking. Like if it was sunny, and the sun is there day after day, then it (the frame) would dry up and crack. The red color helps.

His kayak is the very last one still put together at Kwig.[21] He likes hunting with kayaks. It's been only less than fifteen that he no longer used it. When I was in high school he was still using it. I rode in his kayak once. It was covered with canvas. It's still in Kwig. It's the last one that he made.

He states that nowadays we have outboard motors and Lund aluminum boats. The outboard motor is noisy and when you're hunting, sometimes the animal gets away before you can see it. Or it has more chance of getting away, because of the noise. Back then, when they were hunting with kayaks they had a better chance to come closer to the animal. You have a better chance of spotting, so he thinks it's better to hunt with kayaks.

BILL WILKINSON

I'm from the village Kwigillingok, Alaska, a Yup'ik village. My Yup'ik name is Metervik. It means eagle and was given to me by Frank Andrew, my father-in-law. Years before, I had a name which meant something along the lines of "single eagle" or "lonely eagle." That was a number of people's humor. Frank changed it to something a little more respectful.

One day we were sitting in the kitchen – this is not a mystical thing, I don't really believe it means anything – but I said, "You know Mary Ann, I told you before when I was little, people asked me what I wanted to be." I said, "Well, when I grow up, I want to be an eagle." Then, a couple years after that, I realized you can't grow up to be an eagle. I really did have dreams as a child that I could fly. I could remember I would like fly down my street. I'd be almost waking up. I wasn't awake, but in my dream, if I just moved my arms just the correct way, I could fly right down the street. Sometimes I was like flying across the water. It was really a great feeling. I could sense when I started to wake up, if I didn't move my hands just right, I was like sinking down. That was a bummer!

Eagles, Deck Designs and Kayak Styles
It's ironic, that when I got to Kwig, the school logo is the Kwigillingok Eagles. And my father-in-law's sign inside a kayak on the *ayapervik*, the posts that hold up the *pai* or opening, are eagles. And then his deck design, which we found out years later, is an eagle. We put it on all the traditional boats that we built. There was a big discussion in the family about doing it with this boat because the family design is never to be given away and only passed on through the male side of the family. An exception was made for this museum.

There were originally just a few deck designs in the village, like five to eight. I think we have five written down. Nobody else in the world knows this. They are undocumented. The only deck designs you see are the

...yuk designs. And ...at's it.

...is the style we built ...Kwigillingok over and a ...ins to change in that area a ...around the mouth of the ...ds Tuntutuliak, Eek, Quinhagak, ...news Bay. The area is basically the ...kokwim and the surrounding area. I ...est, most undocumented type of kayak

...yanek, we're in the ...arch stage. We have not written it all down. What we're doing is, we're getting into it totally and traditionally. We're doing it over and over until we get it down rock solid. If you write too early, you're going to make a lot of mistakes. So, we want to build several of these boats. This is our fourth boat. I built three of them before. A lot of work is being done by apprentices. With every boat we build, we get deeper and deeper and deeper. The fifth boat we build will be the ultimate, traditional Caninermiut boat because we'll have the time. We won't have deadlines to worry about.

The grant I wrote to document that is set up to train locals in videography. We want to train locals in editing and buy computer equipment so that we can edit our own material. We feel that the deep understanding of all the nuances of this Caninermiut boat is not documented and it really belongs to the Yup'ik people in that region. We want to be able to have the documentation done by them and with them. We want to train them how to do it, so any information is owned by them. Once we get that well documented, then we want to really open up and share it with the world.

There has been lots of documentary stuff in the village and the Bush over the years. It's very beneficial, but our philosophy is very simple: if we can't document it well, then fine, come in and document it. But if we have the know-how and the technical ability to document it well, we should do it. We should own that, and we should then market that because it's ours. We feel if we can't do that, then it would be a disservice for us not to share it. So, that's how we're kind of operating with all this.

We are dedicating all our time, effort and energy to making sure that we take that knowledge and not just write it down, but we'll take that knowledge and firmly put it into kayak builders' hands. Right now, we're focusing and training Frank's son

Thick and supple from soaking in water, the hide is draped over the kayak frame and readied for cutting and sewing. Following page: Noah Andrew stretches seal skins on the tundra at Kwigillingok.

and his grandson. My children are also his grandsons because I married his daughter. Right now we're putting in much time, effort and energy and we're taking a tremendous financial risk to build a facility and create space. In 1960, when the last traditional mud house went down in the village, it had not been used for some time. When it fell down, there was no space. Because of the population and the economic situation in Kwig, people didn't have extra garages or extra rooms. Everybody was living in everything. So, with the

41

combination of the loss of space and people having modern boats, the demise of the kayak was imminent.

I'm a teacher and I love our school district. We do a great job, but it can't provide the space, day after day, throughout the year, to do this. So we've built a small building, sixteen by twenty-four feet, with our own resources. Within that little building we created four of the most traditionally accurate Caninermiut boats in the world. We're building a twenty-four by sixty foot building now to give our workers a place to build and flourish and train other people. First, we're going to concentrate on training this workforce so there's a direct connection through time immemorial. It may well be economic suicide but it is also a form of deep cultural preservation.

Kayak Construction

The process of construction for this Yup'ik kayak is to build all the parts ahead of time. The actual order of part construction may vary from builder to builder. Once all the parts are made, the gunwales are laid with the cross members notched in. After the bow piece is affixed, the frame is flipped over, affixed to the ground, centered and then ribs and stringers are added. The frame is flipped once again and the forward and aft ridge pieces are added. The center entry circle and stanchions are added last. The skin cover is fitted and attached. Then the deck design is applied.

Frank Andrew's Contributions

At this point in time, the critical issue is Frank's age and his connection. He was raised in a traditional men's house (*qasegiq*). He was raised with kayaks being built all around him throughout the winter. In a modern world, we'd be sitting around watching the TV, doing things at home day after day after day, you know, puzzles, reading or TV. He was building kayaks, watching people building kayaks. He was an apprentice in the most positive, consistent learning environment you could imagine to learn such a thing. It was easy; it was

in the flow of things. It was without crucial pressure, deadlines, and that's a perfect way to learn. That's why he's so good at what he does.

He has an incredible understanding of the timing nuances of the structure of this boat and the chemistry, biology and mathematics are just absolutely unrivaled at this point of time. If you drop just a couple of years below Frank's age – he's eighty-three right now – and you ask other elders in that region, the great majority of the time, they are not going to know the measurement system and the assembly process. They're not going to know the chemistry. They're not going to know the grain orientation, the wood selection, all the biology, and the artistry that goes with it. He knows this stuff like nobody else in the world right now. There may be a few other elders still around that know what he knows. If you look at the boats that are being built, and you go through drawing and connection, every aspect, every part, you can see, when you compare it to the Caninermiut boat, there's a discontinuity there. Just as if a side of a mountain had washed away the surface and you have new deposition going on, there's a broken line that's about ready to occur.

The Kayak as Storyteller

Looking at a kayak is like looking at a bear in the ecosystem. When you look at a bear in the ecosystem, if that bear is not healthy, if it's not intact, then you know something is wrong in the ecosystem, because that means everything below it is really in sad shape. The bear has to depend on everything else. When you examine a kayak, like you would examine a bear in its habitat, you can learn about everything else. When you look at a kayak, it can open up all kinds of windows into understanding Yup'ik culture. For instance, just looking at the paint, it tells you that there was a tremendous amount of trading going on. Some of the paint comes from a hundred and some miles away in Toksook. Some of the paint comes from way down south of Platinum, around a huge point on the side of the cliffs down there. Some of the paint comes from up the Kuskokwim. So there's some trading going on.

Some of the caribou sinew that was used wasn't technically manufactured on the coast. They never made it down there. It was actually constructed up-river. So there's all this trading that goes on. Then if you get into the chemistry and biology and the understanding of those areas, it really gets pretty phenomenal. You're sort of getting into the biological aspect of the skins, and what skin does this and what does that. It's really technical.

Passing It On

What we can pass on to the young people is an appreciation for a national treasure. There's lots of information that has been researched about the pyramids, people who make pyramids; they look back at the Egyptian, Aztec and Mayan. When you look at the Yup'ik people, the kayak, I think, is one of the high points of their technological genius that's overlooked. You look at old photographs and you see an old gray photograph. You don't see the authentic real color when the things were made, which is beautiful and striking. You don't see the really careful carving inside because for the last seventy-five years, more than that, they really didn't do that so very much.

When they finished these boats, they put on their deck designs which are vast and totally undocumented in our area. This design by Frank is the only one documented that I know of in the Kuskokwim region. If you go out there and find those eighty-four year-olds, eighty-three-year-olds, and ask them what deck designs there were in their villages and you seek that stuff out, you're going to find stuff that's undocumented.

Frank Andrew shapes a kayak paddle
at Alaska Native Heritage Center.

I don't think it's in the Smithsonian because missionaries came at a time when there was a transition going on. A little metal had been around for a while and they are cutting corners, and adapting. It's practical to use metal over the wooden pegs and that kind of stuff. But my point is, what we have to offer is, if young people understand the genius of the mathematical system, if they understand the chemistry involved, if they have a biological understanding of a white spruce tree, the trunk and all the wood variations, they'll understand that it is impressive engineering, physics, and a significant cultural accomplishment for all to be proud of.

I've seen some of that intuitive knowledge with Frank. I've seen him do a little bit of looking at the outside of a log, but when we cross-cut the tree, the book is now open. When we split it, we're open for business. He picked up a board last week and looked at it and said, "This thing is going to bend that way." He said, "We need to take off this half an inch right here. You take this half an inch of that particular grain and this thing won't bend." I think it was a day or so later that the board was already bending like he said. So we went and cut off that half inch.

There are certain situations where we cross-cut it at the end grain. When I first started to do this, he looked at me and the grain and I'd say, "Well cool, what are you looking for?" Now, when he and I look at one, because I've worked with him for a while, I'm beginning to see this, and understand this, and see what's here and what's there, just by the end cut of the tree. When we split them, it's like going from a view of your neighborhood when you're walking down the sidewalk to an aerial view like looking down from a

Frank Andrew's old kayak frame rests in
field of Arctic Cotton in Kwigillingok.

plane. You have a total different perspective and it's a lot like diamond cutting.

When we get into the sewing stuff, there's a whole other world there that's really pretty vast. Frank's wife Nellie does some really impressive work. The ladies that came in from Kwig did some incredible work.

Teaching Styles

The traditional way to learn, by watching and listening mainly, is probably one of the best systems in the world. There are many different learning systems. It doesn't mean the modern learning system is automatically bad. It's a fine system for what it has to do. We have this dilemma now where we really don't have time to teach traditionally. We have to pursue a fast track. We have to get these guys, the apprentices, capable as soon as possible. Frank and I are watching them every second. When they make mistakes, we get involved and then we back out. We're aware of the old but we are making some adaptations.

I am aware that asking constant questions is not the traditional way either, but right now, we have to do that. Frank has a sort of Zen-like quality about him. We sit and I just politely ask questions and he just gives answers and I go on. Some of our sessions just go on and on. I ask him these intricate questions and he goes on and on and on. We've had these sitting sessions many times.

The Future

The critical point is the fleeting amount of time that we have left. If we don't transfer what Frank knows now, there will not be a generation after him who will ever know it again. No matter how hard we try, no matter how hard we study and build these boats, we will never really know all that he knows.

A final point is in this year, the year 2000, there are elders who are Frank's age, eighty-two and eighty-three. We have just those few years of this particular group, and after that, there aren't any more of totally tradi-

tionally trained elders. When that particular group of elders that were trained in the traditional houses is gone, from then on out we're just imagining what it was and what they knew. This year is when we – as a population and as a country – have to rally and dig in and sit down with our tape recorders every time they talk, and listen to everything they say. You have to ask a lot of questions. If I hadn't asked a question about kayak building, we wouldn't be where we are today. My wife, just the other day, said, "I can't believe what my mother knows." They worked for four days, five women, every day and all they did at that point was prepare the thread to get ready to sew the kayak. And they aren't even using the traditional sinew. We're doing that on the next boat. That's going to be a whole other level.

This is the year 2000 and we may have three, we may have five and if we are really lucky, ten years, but after that, it's over.

MARY ANN WILKINSON

I am the daughter of Frank and Nellie Andrew. My mother was the main instructor for the skin sewing and I am one of the apprentices. I had never sewn a skin boat before. I was a little nervous, but mother did a good job instructing us.

It took five seal skins to cover the kayak. They caught them this year. They are this year's seals. To sew them, we use what Mother calls *yualuq*. I don't know the English word for it. There are two types of threads we prepared. One of them took us about three days to make. They're not so long and we have to prepare them a special way. They aren't covered with wax. The others are about two arm lengths. That would be like two-and-one-half yards long. How we prepare them is we braid them loosely but not too loosely and not so tight. The end where the needle comes through is prepared with a different kind of thread and it is connected to the waxed thread.

Noah Andrew and brother-in-law Bill Wilkinson collect driftwood
along the Kuskokwim River for the curved bow and stern pieces that
are so critical for strength in constructing the frame of the kayak.

In the old days, they used sinew. It came from the back muscle of a reindeer or a caribou. They used to let the nape hang so that the blood drips out and then they scrape the meat off. Back home we have a sample of it. I can't believe it's so thin, I mean probably as thin as my fingernail, the strands. They take three strands and braid them. Back then, down at the coastal area, they didn't have reindeer so they used to trade with people up where there's reindeer. There's people that prepared sinews and from what Pop said, some of them used to insert a strand of the inside bark of a willow tree. They take a strand of that and insert it in the middle of the sinews.

When I asked my mother how they used to prepare those, she didn't know because she said they used to trade. The other sinew they used is from beluga whale.

I think the skin sewing was done by both men and women. The women have to sew the five parts. I think there are two at the bottom and then you pattern it. You've seen skins that are dried; they have holes around them where they stretch them out. You have to remove that outside layer and remove the holes so there's a straight line going across, so that you can sew it to the other sealskin.

We sew the skins together using a special stitch. You don't pull it tight because if you pull it tight, when it dries up it will be too tight. Then after you sew it, in and out, you reverse it and you put grass in there and make a whipstitch. The grass soaks up water and makes the seam waterproof like in the gut parkas. We start sewing in the morning and sew all day and all night. We can't let it sit overnight.

Before we launch the boat, we have this substance that is dried moss and we mix it with seal oil. Then you spread it and it becomes green and gooey like glue, and you put that along the seams to seal them.

Once the skins are attached together, we lay the skin down on the top of the frame and it is brought up and tacked into place. Once that's done, the men take over.

For preparing the skins, the meat and the hair is taken off. Then traditionally, to soften the skin, they used urine, only male urine. I think it softens the skins and it stretches much easier and probably takes care of the oily stuff too. I'm not sure.

When I was growing up, we were taught to watch and learn, don't ask why. My father is very flexible and Bill asks him a whole lot of questions, sometimes the same question again in two weeks or a month after. Pop's got this incredible patience and he once said that for one to learn, one has to ask. Once someone made the comment, "Your son-in-law asks a lot of questions." That's how he got started with the kayaks though.

I'm glad I'm having this experience, the opportunity to be involved in this traditional kayak. I'm anxious, yet at the same time, I'm excited as I'm learning.

NOAH ANDREW SR.

I am Frank Andrew's son. I was born in 1951 in Kwigillingok. I'm forty-nine. In Yup'ik they call me Aiggalnguq. For short they call me Ike.

I'm the apprentice and I'm learning. I've learned quite a bit already about kayak making. This is my first year fully employed under *Qayanek* in Kwig. *Qayanek* started maybe two years ago. My dad's old kayak was at the school and we used that as a guide to make what we should be making. We also asked my dad some questions that we are not sure of, like what kind of wood we should use.

To me, if we weren't doing kayak building now, and my dad and the elders were gone, we would probably have lost one of our traditional values. It's a good thing we are doing it now because they're telling us what the names are. Even I, and the other folks older than I, aren't used to the part names.

My dad is one of the people that know about kayak parts. He was the only one in our village which I remember that was using kayaks even though the other people were using boats and outboard motors. I used to see him travel quite a ways with my mom in the back and my uncle in another kayak. During springtime, they used to leave and they are out there maybe a week or two, paddling out wherever they want to go.

The kayaks we're building now, can carry at least four people: one in the front, one in the back and two in the middle, one facing forward and the other facing back. My mom would be facing back. That's how they used to travel.

The materials for this kayak are mostly spruce and some yellow cedar, due to seasonal wood collection problems. There's no trees where I came from, no trees at all. So, we have to look for parts that we need along the coast, or we have to go up through the mouth of the Kuskokwim to see if we can find good wood we can use for making kayaks. The other parts, the long parts, probably in the old days, I don't know how they used to get them, but they probably had to go up and search for those like *apamak* which are those real long pieces. It has to be one long piece, all the way from the front to the back. Those probably were the hardest pieces of wood to find. The kayak that we made here, the wood for that was flown from Seattle. The gunwales are yellow cedar.

There's two different colors probably to use. If they are making that kayak for me, and if it's my first kayak, they would've colored it gray. My second kayak would be colored this red color.

My dad had another color that he uses for the paddles and hunting implements. I think it's black, like that double paddle they are using.

In preparing the skins, the ladies take all the meat and fat off, and then when the oil is all taken away from the skin, they wrap it and put it in the corner some place. They let it stay there for a while, maybe a week, and then the hair will peel off.

The men do the stretching and drying of the skin. They take the fur off, wash it and stretch it, and they take the oil off. They use the *uluaq* to scrape it off. We use sticks to stretch the skins. My dad always does that.

Eighty-three-year-old Frank Andrew takes to the waters of Kachemak Bay in his traditional skin-covered kayak to the applause of the crowd on shore.

Central Yup'ik Qayaq

Length: 15' 8"   Width: 32"   Depth: 17"   Weight: 65 lbs.
Materials: Spruce wood frame, sealskin cover, natural stains

Master boat builder: Phillip Moses, Toksook Bay, Alaska
Apprentices: George Nevak, John Alirkar
Skin sewers: Maria Moses, Martina Chagluak, Julia Nevak, Sophie Agimuk, Rachel Mitchell

PHILLIP MOSES
Translated from Central Yup'ik by Vernon Chimegalrea.

My Yup'ik name is Nurataq. It isn't my given Yup'ik name. My given Yup'ik name is Minegtuli. In the Yup'ik tradition, whenever a person has died, that person's name was passed on to a living relative. That is why I go by that name. I was born in Nightmute. I was born during the season of plants (summer) 1925. Since that time period, this (Toksook Bay) has been my home and I have never lived anywhere else.

I was taught how to build kayaks by my uncles. It was like they were my school instructors. I would tire-lessly work on the ribs of the kayak. I work on two kayaks at the same time with them. As they became elderly men, I would assist them as they instructed me, doing the tasks they had to do like using the adz to smooth out the wood. They would then do the finishing touches. I would assist them until the completion of the project. I have the two kayaks that they made, the two that I worked on and learned from. They are, however, deteriorating as they are so old.

The men in those days tried not to be without a kayak. Even though some of them were not as fortunate as others, they always had a kayak. Their peers would help those who could not provide for a kayak. Also they

Phillip Moses and David Alirkar, hunting partners, work on their kayak.

made sure they had kayaks, as they didn't have any (other) boats. Their kayak was their source of getting food. They used it for many purposes. Also in the spring, they would use it down in the ocean to hunt seals.

The kayak was a source for living. They used it for hunting. They were always using it for subsistence. The kayaks would be completely outfitted with hunting implements. They used them to travel into the wilderness. They would especially use them in the spring. They would be outfitted with implements to hunt, including implements to get seals.

They would help that person making a kayak as they were all congregated in the men's house (*qasegiq*). If a person did not have something, one of the men would give it to him. The bearded sealskins were usually used. They would use those when they were available. They would use the best of that type. If they were not available, they would use spotted seal for the surface area. They would also use old seal pokes if they didn't have anything else.

They used to travel great distances. I also know of more than one instance where they would travel to Bethel to purchase tea or tobacco. I heard of a couple instances of trips taking them days because it is such a great distance. Those are instances of places they had gone great distances.

Up to this day, whenever I think of it, they had a hard life using kayaks. I know that for a fact to this day. That is how I see it. I too travel out to sea just prior to the kayak no longer being used, during that time when they were still using kayaks.

For kayak skins, if they didn't have skins from the previous year they would use skins from two-year-old bearded seals (two-year-old seals have hardly any fur on them) because they were thick skinned. They would scrape the hair off when they used those skins that had hardly any fur. Also, the less fortunate would use the skins of walrus. They would make the skin thinner and use them for (kayak) skins. Those who just didn't have skins would help each other and complete the kayaks.

The less fortunate, whenever they didn't have the stains, would use charcoal from the men's house and grind it up and use it as a stain on the kayak. However those who had it would always make an effort to use red ochre on the ribs of the kayak. For the implements that are going to be on top of the kayak, they would use blue, the blue clay. They were called *qesuuraq*. They made an effort to paint it with such. They would also make designs using a black clay. They used this dark black rock which was called *avisgar*.

They would carefully paint designs on them, trying their best to make their kayaks attractive. They would be designs with their emblems, however nowadays they don't pay much attention to detail. They would also use white clay (*urasqaq*). Traditionally they would make a compound using the white clay to caulk the seams. They would use *urasqaq* when they developed cracks. Those are things they would use at the time. That is what they would use as compounds when the seams opened up. That is what they would use to stain them. They also used (seal) oil. They would let become rancid (and sticky). That is what they did.

The red stain is the other color besides the blue. Up

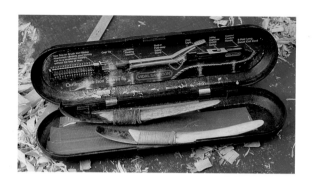

Phillip Moses stretches skin over kayak frame and cuts away
excess material. Top: Phillip's toolbox. Left: Lashing the cockpit
to the frame. Following page: Men and women work together
to cut and tack skins over kayak frame.

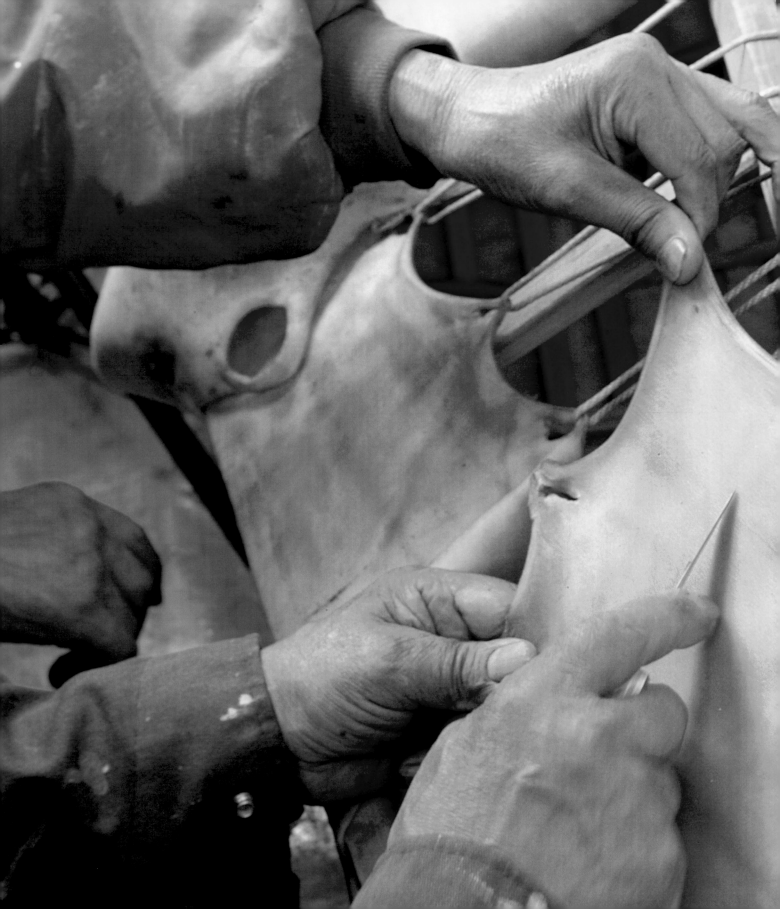

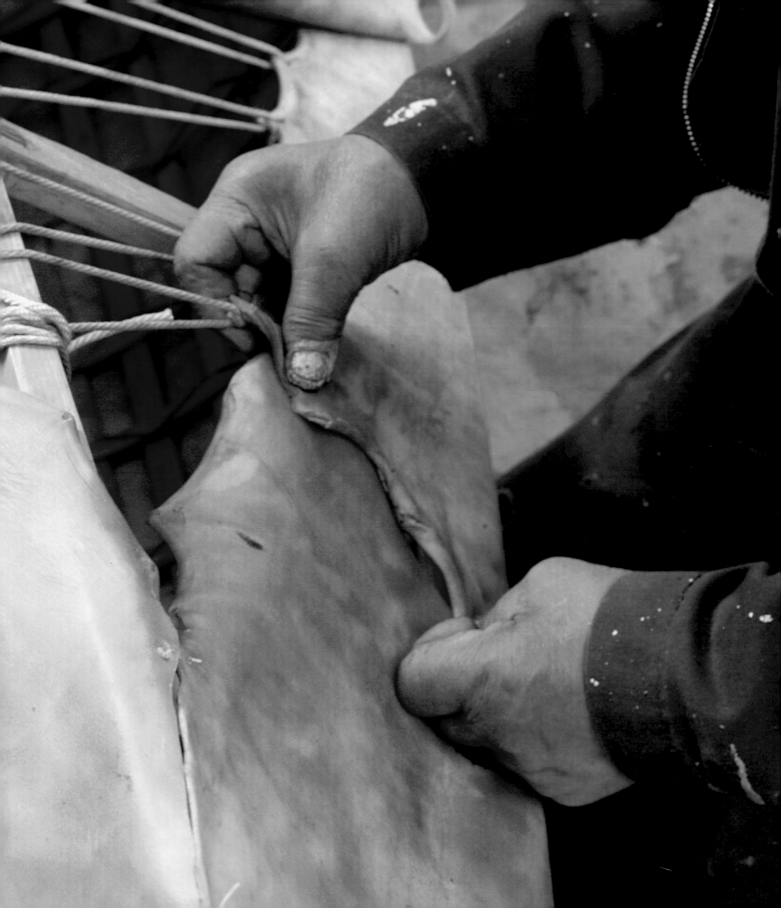

there, near here, right across, there is where it is found. From what I know there are two. The red color is called *uiteraq*. Then, down the coast at the point is where the *uiteraq* is located. It cannot be harvested in great amounts. It is located up on a ledge. They would shoot at it trying to make it fall is what I hear (is how they get it). That is what they made an effort to paint their paddles and kayak sleds with. It was like this: they couldn't use the red ochre on their paddles or on their gaffs, especially in the ocean. That is what their tradition was. They were instructed not to use it as a stain because the animals, the seal, were afraid of the color red.

Whenever the kayaks became old and their ribs began to break, they would take the skin off and repair the ribs of the kayak. They would put braces on the broken parts. They would repair the parts that they could, that is what I observed. They would only repair them in the spring, taking them into the men's house (*qasegiq*), here in Umkumiut.

The kayak was those ancestors' who resided in these small communities tradition. If someone, for some reason, did not have a kayak, they would be in trouble; they would not be able to hunt. He would not be able to provide for his family. They used it from summer until winter. That was their tradition. They used it as their mode of transportation throughout the wilderness. They would bring along their children, those they could bring along, through this term *alrapak* (sitting back-to-back). In my thoughts, this would allow them knowledge (on kayak) traveling when they did this. It was a form of teaching them.

Also they never just left them (the kayaks) lying around. They would take good care of them, making sure the skin would not rot. They would take great care so that they would not be lying wet and rotting. They took great care of them so they did not deteriorate prematurely. They were told to store them properly. They were instructed by the elder men to take care of them so they would have something to use the following spring. Some people, although they might have one

from the previous year, make other implements for use. They would make paddles, gaffs; that is what they would do.

I've heard of stories about women, should they have orphaned children, where their grandmothers would make them kayaks. I don't know how they being women made kayaks.

Some people told stories of kayaks and kayaking. They would tell of trips. The stories I heard are from time immemorial. Since the kayak has been with the Yup'ik peoples from those ancestors of ours, our stories and legends would tell of kayaks. They made sure no one was without a kayak and it was a practice to make the grandchildren kayaks. It was even a tradition among the women to make kayaks.

It was more than once that I heard about how they made an effort to use tree stumps for the stern and the bow and also the surface supporters. They would use wood that was tough, but yet pliable, the type they could bend and make into drum frames. That is what they would use. Since wood was one of their resources, those ancestors of ours knew the certain types of wood to use. They knew the type of wood that would be straight-grained. They would use whatever wood was around. They never had that much either; whatever wood that drifted in was like a gift to them.

I was glad when I served as the leader in the kayak crew. I was a little hesitant at first; I was a little unsure of actually building a kayak at first, although I had my apprentices. However, I am happy about it. It was like I was in school. I was satisfied with my completed project. It was like bringing back a Yup'ik art form that was lost. Also, since it was my first experience to complete a kayak, it improved my ability to make a kayak. The time spent in Anchorage greatly improved my knowledge of kayak-building, giving me more confidence about building another kayak. I have a good feeling that should I build another kayak. That is what I am grateful for.

Sophie Agimuk of Toksook Bay weaves
a grass mat for the bottom of the kayak.

Aleut (Unangan) Ulûxtax
(Double hatch Kayak)

Length: 21'   Width: 2'   Depth: 13"   Weight: 70 lbs.
Materials: Spruce, red cedar and oak frame, sea lion and bearded sealskin covering

Master boat builder: Mike Livingston, Anchorage, Alaska, originally Cold Bay, Alaska
Apprentices: Hope Morris, Eddie Evan, Helena Pagano
Skin sewers: Grace Harrod, June Simeonoff Pardue

Mike Livingston's story of how he came to learn about his heritage, and then used the kayak as an instrument for immersion, is one that is told with variations by many Alaska Native people today. The cultural disruption that occurred with European contact had wide-reaching effects on the members of the indigenous cultures that had lived in Alaska for, at the very least, ten thousand years prior to this intrusion. Also, many parents felt they were doing an injustice to their children if they tried to raise them within a traditional cultural framework. The indigenous languages became almost lost and, without the language, transmitting cultural ways and values becomes a most difficult task.

The traditional technology of boat building is a rich instrument for revitalizing many aspects of the culture. Accompanying the techniques and skills are the stories.

Embedded in the stories are keys to regaining cultural knowledge and making it useful for today.

In the quest for immersing himself in the culture of his ancestors, Mike gathered a group of young, very enthusiastic helpers to work on his boat. He has a gift for relating to youth, gathering them around him. First, they covered a frame with nylon and then made a second which they covered the traditional way, with sealskin. When they were working, they were a dedicated group, as indicated in their interviews. His enthusiasm spread to each and every one of his students. Herein lies the future of boat building.

Journal entry excerpts for this project reflect the interaction and sharing that took place between the boat builders who came from different Alaska Native cultural groups.

Mike Livingston's Journal

May 21 – Got a phone call from my dad in Chignik saying he had a good tip for me on de-hairing skins: lime. The lime is caustic, same as wood ashes. You soak the skins in lime and water, stirring it regularly until the hair begins to slip. You may want to remove the epidermis. Pa remembers looking at kayaks in Chenega in April 1950 and they looked like they still had the epidermis on them. They're all gone now, wiped out by the earthquake (tsunami). The next process is to wash the skin in a washer machine with a little soap. Then wash with a little vinegar to bring the pH back to seven. Pa looked at the skins in Chenega and they looked like overhand stitch, edge to edge. They take them (the kayaks) out of the water every five days and oil them with seal or fish oil.

May 22 – Met with the three Yup'ik kayak builders today from Toksook Bay. The two older men were sitting flat on the concrete floor in perfect kayak positions, planing down their gunwales.

May 23 – Watched Gregor and Nick bend the cockpit coaming for their kayak. They sure have much nicer wood than I was able to get. It is knot-free, straight-grained, soft and light. My wood has knots, looks like a crummy two-by-four. Gregor kindly agreed to sell me one of his extra pieces of spruce. Gregor came by today and showed me his photo album. The man can do some impressive woodwork. It's pretty clear he understands how the ancients built baidarkas and why they built them the way they did.

May 30 – Wayne was nice to loan Hope and me some eighteen-foot-long red cedar planks to set our gunwales upon.

Mike Livingston inspects driftwood for use in his kayak on the beach at St. Paul. Following page: St. Paul village on St. Paul Island in the Pribilofs.

July 8 – Hope and I began this morning by taking a twenty-foot-long board and ripping into strips for stringers. Then I borrowed the wood steamer, which the Yup'ik kayak team had made out of a metal coffee can, and several sections of stovepipe. Hope and I moved the frame out to the site and I began steaming and cutting ribs.

August 11 – But, gosh this whole ordeal of de-hairing the sea lion hides sure is stinky.

August 29 – Test floated the baidarka. It floated, didn't leak a drop! Hope and I made a pretty good paddling team.

Hope Morris' Journal

August 4 – I watched the Yup'ik team from Kwig sew sealskins. I learned a lot. They showed us how to braid and make leads so that they can fit into smaller needles.

August 12 – We finished the last of the planing; I planed down the stern plank. Then we started staining, sheesh, what a long process. Seems like it would be easy 'til you start. Our kayak is beautiful, long and sleek.

August 22 - Today was the day. We got the entire boat sewed up. It is covered in skin and it looks great. We will have to wax it when it's dry, but for the most part it's all done. Yeah!

Eddie Evan's Journal

So far I've learned that Aleut baidarkas are longer, shallower and narrower than the Eskimo-style kayaks. They are fun to create and are a blast in the water! What excites me most about this project is sewing on the sealskin. I realize it will definitely be a task, but I am looking forward to it. I've always known the basics of my culture, but never really did any research. All I have are the stories my relatives pass on to me.

MIKE LIVINGSTON

I was born in 1957 in Fort Collins, Colorado, and raised in Cold Bay, Alaska. My mother is Aleut and my father is white. My mother was born and raised in the Prince William Sound area. My father was born and raised in Kansas.

When my grandmother was raised in the Prince William Sound area in the early 1900s, it wasn't particularly cool to be Native back then. The Native ways were shunned and my grandmother was discouraged from doing anything Native. So was my mother. My mother was discouraged from learning the old language or learning any old Native ways, or doing anything that was Native. For example, my grandmother told my mother never to ride in a baidarka. One night, my mom needed a ride home across a lake or a bay or a stream, and she ended up getting into a baidarka. When she got home she said she opened up the door to her home and she saw stars. The instant she walked in the door of my grandmother's home, my grandmother could tell from the smell of the skins that she had been in a baidarka. It so upset my grandmother that she hit my mother so hard, my mother saw stars.

So, when I was born in the 1950s, my mother had evidently been exposed to a great deal of discrimination and racism against Alaska Natives. It was so much to the point that probably when she decided to choose a husband, she went out of her way to choose a white man so her kids wouldn't be exposed to the racism and the discrimination against Alaska Natives. It was so much so that when I was born, my mom put down on my birth certificate that my race was white and so was hers.

It wasn't until I was in my early teens, I was told I am Alaska Native, and then there was a lot of confusion in my life. Why hadn't I been told earlier? What is an Alaskan Native? What is an Aleut? For a while I just kind of ignored the question. When I was in college in Minnesota, people would ask me where I was from. I

would tell them, "I'm from Alaska." They'd say, "Are you Eskimo?" I'd say, "No I'm Aleut," and they'd say, "What's an Aleut?" and I'd say, "I don't really know."

So for me it became kind of a quest to find out what an Aleut is. And the baidarka, the Aleut kayak, became a vehicle for me to learn more about the culture of my ancestors. I'm talking about the ancient culture as it existed before the Russians arrived in Alaska in the 1700s. That was what I wanted to learn most about.

I went back to Cordova, met my grandmother and spent some time with her before she passed away. When I was in Cordova, I kayaked a little bit in the lake there. When I was a kid I had done some kayaking in Cold Bay, but I hadn't made the connection yet. And then in 1978 I moved out to Unalaska, in the Aleutian Islands, with the Unalaska High School Baidarka Building Project. I worked with a couple of older Aleuts there, Phil Tutiakoff and Bill Cherapanoff. Bill had made a lot of model baidarkas. It was a good project, but it was frustrating because we all wanted to do it the traditional way, the ancient way, with stone tools and stuff like that, but we didn't know what to do. So every time we picked up a modern-day tool, a hatchet or chisel, it was like no, we can't do that because it's not traditional. We didn't end up completing a baidarka in that project.

I ended up going back to Cold Bay and on my own, experimenting with wood, I was able to get a frame completed. I lived in Unalaska for a few years and ended up moving to Anchorage, built a couple more frames. Then, in 1999, I came out to the Heritage Center for the first time and was really impressed with what they are doing out here. In January of this year I started making a frame for a one-hatch baidarka.

To date, I've made one frame in Cold Bay, two here in Anchorage, a one-hatch and a three-hatch, and then one here at the Heritage Center. I did twenty-two years of research, at times fairly intense, roughly from 1978 to 2000.

Mike Livingston, wearing traditional parka and hat,
paddles a kayak in the waters off St. Paul Island.

Apprentice Hope Morris wears a
traditional Alutiiq beaded headdress.

When I first began this quest to learn more about the ancient Aleut culture, some of the stuff I found out was kind of disturbing. I didn't know anything about Aleut history, but in a nutshell what I learned was that there was an ancient culture that lived in the Aleutian Islands for thousands and thousands of years, maybe ten, fifteen thousand years. We don't know how many people lived in the Aleutian Islands, but say it was twenty thousand people that were there when the Russians arrived in 1741. In short order, the Russians obliterated that population, that culture and, from what I understand, the population went from say twenty thousand down to two thousand people in less than fifty years. A lot of that ancient culture was destroyed. A lot of the stories were gone, a lot of the boat building techniques – why they built boats the way they did – lost forever. The language was changed, and the continuity of passing boat building from generation to generation, from father to son and grandfather to grandson, in my opinion, has been lost forever.

So I've tried to find older Aleuts that knew how to build baidarkas, but basically I wasn't able to find anybody who had learned how to build baidarkas from their fathers or grandfathers. So what I was forced to do was to learn what I could from books, from photographs of frames, the few baidarka frames that are in museums throughout the world. I contacted people like David Zimmerly out of Canada, Derek Hutchinson from Great Britain, a world famous sea kayaker, George Dyson, out of Canada and now Bellingham, Washington. Then I had to take whatever information I could gather from around the world and take wood, and tools, modern wood and modern tools, and experiment. I had to learn the basic parts of the frame, the gunwales, thwarts, keelson, ribs and stringers, and try to learn how those were built, and just build them. The more frames I built and covered and paddled, the more I learned about ancient Aleut baidarka construction. So a lot of the songs and what we call poems, the old boat building style – why they built the parts of the kayak

the way that they did – are, in my opinion, lost secrets.

The boat that we've built here is an Aleut-style kayak. There are a lot of different words for the Aleut kayak. There is an ancient word for the kayak; it's something like *ulûxtax*. And that's probably not even so much an ancient word as it is a Russian-influenced word. It means a two-hatch kayak. The one-hatch kayak was something like *iqyax*. Then there's the Russian-Aleut word which is *baidarka*. Then, of course, the modern day word is kayak.

Construction

Aleut kayaks were not really cargo ships. They were more like racing hulls. They weren't designed to carry a bunch of weight; they were designed to get from point A to point B, point A usually being the beach and point B being the sea otter or seal. Their purpose was for getting there quickly, making the kill, and returning to shore. They were hunting machines, hunting tools.

The boat that we built is a two-hatch kayak; two people can sit in it. It's got a wooden frame, made out of the smallest possible pieces of wood. You start with the gunwales, the two side pieces, and you spread those with the thwarts. You flop it upside-down, put in the ribs and attach the stringers. At least this is the way I build it. I'm not saying this is the right way, but the way I build it. Then I turn the kayak back right-side-up, and put in the cockpit coamings, the stanchions, and the deck beams. Then I flop it, turn it upside-down again, and put in the bow piece, then the stern plank and then the keelson.

As far as the wood that was used, in ancient times the Aleuts, the Unangan from the Aleutian Islands, used whatever driftwood came to the Aleutian Islands as well as the little wood that grows there such as alder. I was in St. Paul recently and they have what they call "trees" that grow there, but they look more like roots in the ground and don't stick up. But in Cold Bay and Unalaska, there's alder. Green wood bends a lot easier than dried wood. But for this baidarka, I used spruce for the gunwales and stringers; for the thwarts, red cedar; for the ribs, oak; for the bow piece, I used a spruce root; and for the stern plank, I think red cedar. The keelson is of spruce.

In ancient times, the frames were lashed together with sinew. I also read baleen, whatever was locally available. We couldn't come up with sinew in time, or within our budget, so we ended up using fake sinew to tie it together. In the really ancient frames, no metal was used to fasten it together. We didn't use any metal either.

I don't know whether or not in ancient times any glue was used. It certainly could've been made out of something that I'm not aware of. In making the cockpit coamings we did use some glue to fasten the hoops together. Then we used some glue in the bow piece to peg in the bow piece and the stern piece.

I wanted this frame to last a long time, and I know that in the ancient times they really knew how to take good care of a kayak frame. They knew how to handle it; they knew what parts were strong, and what parts were weak. Today I watch people pick up the frames. They lift it up from parts you are not supposed to, and so I intentionally made this frame a little stronger. A lot of people like picking up the kayak by the bow plate. Traditionally, they probably were not picked up by the bow plate, so I strengthened that up some with glue and pegs. Some think the hole in the Yup'ik kayaks is for picking the kayak up. I wouldn't use that for lifting. I think it's probably to lighten the load. I know lightness and flexibility were very important components in the Aleut kayak. There is a world of difference between a rigid fiberglass kayak and a flexible frame.

In my opinion, the way to pick up the kayak is by putting your arm all the way around it to where you're grasping the keel. But the worst place to pick up the old style of kayak frames, baidarka frames, was by the bow pieces because there were so many pieces that were just basically lashed together. You yank on that bow plate and you can snap it off.

In terms of the covering, in the past I've used canvas,

or nylon and they are both really nice to work with. They are inexpensive to buy, and easy to sew. I've also worked a little bit with a nylon airplane fabric. The nylon from one of the other kayaks was from George Dyson. I used eight-ounce nylon that I waterproofed with beeswax and paraffin. You melt the beeswax and the paraffin together and paint it on with a brush, take a normal clothes iron, and that melts the glue into the eight-ounce nylon. It ends up slightly yellowish so it kind of looks like real hide.

The Skins

When I started to get interested in this project, I was told I needed to find a master skin sewer who knew how to sew sea lion hides, or seal hides onto baidarka frames. People would give me a list of names and villages to call up and down the Aleutian Islands and the Alaska Peninsula. I'd finally locate these numbers and locate these people and ask them, "Have you sewn a sea lion or seal hide on to a baidarka?" "No, I haven't." So then I'd go back and get more names and phone numbers. Long story made short: I think there is only about a dozen people, a dozen Aleuts, that know how make baidarka frames and only maybe about five people that know how to sew the skins on to the kayak. So in this kayak the frame is important, but in my mind what is more important is trying to learn how to work with the hides, how to sew the hides on. I hadn't done that and neither had my apprentices.

I had the privilege of watching the Yup'ik from Kwig sew their skins onto their kayak and I've learned a tremendous amount from them. I know there is a difference between Yup'ik and Aleut, but there are probably a lot of similarities too. I got some sea lion hides from St. Paul that the people out there collected and were nice enough to part with. I've learned some of the process for de-hairing those.

There's a whole art, once the seal or sea lion is killed, to skinning it carefully so that you don't cut big holes in the hides. There's a whole art to de-fatting the hide and de-hairing the hide, and there's an art to stretching it and getting it prepared for the kayak. I learned a little bit of that process when I was on St. Paul Island in the Pribilof Islands. I learned a little bit more of that process when I was working with the Yup'ik from Kwig.

It's like a mystery; it's like a puzzle where all the pieces have been scattered throughout the world and, over time, those pieces to the puzzle have deteriorated and it's an intriguing mystery to try to put together. You have to have a lot of patience and persistence and detective skills to try to reassemble that.

Spiritual and Protective Designs

I read one book where they said they had a spirit line on the inside of the gunwales. I haven't yet had the luxury of going to museums and actually putting my hands on old frames. I've looked at the old frames in the Baranof Museum on Kodiak Island. I've seen photographs of the baidarka frame in the Lowie Museum at the University of California, Berkeley, but I haven't actually gone and put my hands on them. Hopefully, I'll be able to do that in the near future and, I think when I do, I'll learn a tremendous amount more now that I've built some frames.

I've seen some carvings on the cockpit stanchions. I had to laugh a little bit when we were finishing up the baidarka. One of my apprentices, Eddie Evan, was carving on that particular part of the boat. I said, "Eddie we're supposed to be painting that. What are you doing carving on that?" Eddie is eighteen years old and, like most eighteen-year-olds, is somewhat impatient at times. He was carving his initials on that part of the boat.

Mike Livingston shows John Merculief how to balance a kayak in St. Paul.

The last thing we did on the frame was to paint it. Traditionally, they were painted with red ochre, exactly why, I haven't heard or don't understand yet. We've painted it with a natural cherry stain that was a combination of stain and Varathane.

Apprentices

My first apprentice, Eddie Evan, is eighteen years old. He's Iñupiat. He's a very energetic young man who's willing to learn, and willing to learn about other cultures also. I've been honored to have Eddie here working with me. He's a good worker.

My second apprentice is Hope Morris. Hope is my niece and she's Alutiiq from Kodiak Island. I've had some skin sewing apprentices like Helena Pagano. Helena is eighteen and she's Aleut. Her ancestors are from Attu Island.

I use a combination of the western and traditional way of teaching. In ancient times, a father might show his son how to use stone tools. Actually, the instruction would probably start shortly after birth, flexibility for the Aleut boys in terms of using the kayak and so forth. Then one could do education over a long time period, hands-on stuff. With my apprentices, safety is of utmost importance. I don't want them to be working on a table saw and cut some fingers or a hand off. So basically I do all the machine tool work. They are tortured into watching me do all that work. They may want to use table saw or a band saw. Maybe, if they apprentice with me for a year or two, or three, they can learn about shop safety and learn how dangerous the wood working tools can be. Once the sharper work has been done, they do the sanding and use the hand tools and do the planing. I'm sure that they are a little bit frustrated by not being able to do more, but if nothing else, they learn by watching the process, by seeing how the parts are made. I've tried to teach them the English terms: the gunwales, the thwarts, the stringers, the keelson, as well as the Aleut words for the different parts. We may not have the exact correct pronunciation down on those words, but we try to learn them.

Baidarka building is a concept. You take a bunch of tiny little parts of wood as small as you can possibly get them, you lash them together and then you cover it with the hide. The hide is a structural member of the kayak. It helps hold it together. So it's all an engineering feat and an engineering mystery in terms of how they were able to paddle as quickly as they were on such long distances and so forth.

This Project
Working at the Heritage Center has been a wonderful process this summer, sharing some of those mysteries and those puzzle parts with other people and trying to reassemble what the baidarka represented to Aleuts. It's hard for anybody to imagine. It's like, in today's society, it's as important as the automobile, and so for me, building the baidarka has been kind of a time travel to learn about the culture of my ancestors as it existed a short three hundred years ago.

I guess one thing I want to emphasize is that three hundred years ago, a hundred percent of the people that lived in Aleut territory knew about baidarkas. Every man, woman and child knew how important they were. They knew basically how they were made, and they knew basically how the skins were sewn on. Today, probably only one-tenth of one percent of the people that live in Aleut territory really know how to make baidarkas. Some people might say, "Well, three hundred years, that's a long time," and in a sense, it is. Yet in another sense, it's not at all if you look at how many thousands of years Aleuts lived in the Aleutian Islands. It's a drop in the bucket

When I was out on St. Paul, I found an Aleut dictionary and found the ultimate Aleut insult: "You're dad doesn't even own a baidarka!"

That really shows how important they were to the culture. It would be comparable today to "Your dad doesn't even own a car."

The Future
I'm really concerned about the future. It's been decades, if not more than decades, since the last baidarka was built. I don't know the exact time frame. It might be over a century the last baidarka was built which was covered with the sea lion or sealskin. On the one hand, I'm really inspired by the boat-building project at the Heritage Center; we've got a tremendous amount of momentum. But my concern is that momentum will be completely lost. For example, this year I built two baidarkas, started one January first, got it done, started another one. We've got the frame done now. I'm just really concerned that the momentum will be lost and the interest will wane and it will be another hundred years before another baidarka is built.

As soon as I'm done with this one, I'd like to start on a third one for this year. So far I really haven't found someone or someplace that's interested in that. As part of my continuing education, I'd like to go to Kwig and work with them for a while. They have a school there. But so far, I haven't found another place. There are a lot of people who are interested in baidarkas, but they don't realize the time commitment it takes. For example, I had an invitation to a village. They wanted me to fly out to their community and build a baidarka in a day! A day is just not enough time. The first one this year took me six months. The second one is taking me three months, weekends and evenings.

A lot of people in today's American society of the twenty-first century may see absolutely no value in an old culture that is basically extinct. But, in my mind, there is a lot that can be learned from baidarka building and baidarka paddling. It's hard to describe exactly what that is, but it's perhaps slowing down, learning some really old ways, and learning respect for the ocean, respect for the sea life that's in the ocean, and the respect for a people who were able to survive in some of the most harsh and most beautiful weather in the world.

The weather doesn't get much worse than in the Aleutian Islands. But, they were able to survive and thrive for many years, more years than the American society has been around. They were able to live there happily and to do well. I think there is a lot to be learned there. The more projects we have like this, the better chance we have of learning some of those concepts.

EDDIE EVAN

I am an urban Native. I'm eighteen. My last name is my mother's maiden name which comes from my grandfather. I was born here and raised here in Anchorage and never really left here. My mom is originally from Nome. I have a lot of aunts in Unalakleet and Shaktoolik.

I was pretty psyched about getting aboard this project because nowadays it's like people don't make things anymore; they buy them. This is a lot of fun learning about how it was back then, how hard it could be.

I found out about the project because the Heritage Center offers courses to Native high school students two hours every day, after school. I took the *atlatl*[22] and spear-making class. I ran into Mike and he asked if I'd like to be an apprentice even though he's Aleut and I'm Iñupiat. He invited me and I was willing to do it.

In working on this boat, I like the planing. You get down to a certain form before you can put the skin on. We (the apprentices) planed everything down to the shape except for the gunwales. We just put holes in those. Everything has to fit so it's a challenge. It's pretty time consuming but the effort shows.

I've learned that the Aleuts were very ingenious.

They had ideas back then that marvel modern man. Like the bow, for example, scientists are still trying to figure out how they came up with that idea, the cutwater, and the shock absorption and how they made them so light. These are very lightweight.

I'm just glad I got to do this. Mike is a good guy. I haven't seen him mad yet. He interprets everything so I can understand. I'm more of a visual person, if I see you do it once, I won't forget. There is an old Chinese proverb that says, " Tell me and I'll forget; show me, I may remember; but let me do it and I'll never forget."

HOPE MORRIS

I am from Old Harbor, which is a village on Kodiak Island. Right now, I live here in Anchorage. We just moved about four months ago. I'm twenty-four. I am married and I have two kids.

I am Alutiiq. All my life I was Aleut, and all of a sudden, I find out I'm Alutiiq.[23] But see, I really didn't believe it. People can call me what they want, but I know what I am. My grandma says we are a different culture. She says that she can hardly understand the Aleuts on the Chain, but she can understand the Yup'ik. So, I have come to realize we are not the Aleut. We're close relatives, but not Aleut.

I am the oldest great-granddaughter of Larry Matfay.[24] I gave him his first great-great-grandchild. When I think of his send-off, they sang. It wasn't just a cry, it was a sob. I've never felt that. I don't know what the word was, that kind of pain; it was just so emotional. One of the elders sang, she sang, it was more like a howl, you know, it was so sad.

I regret all the years that he tried to talk to us. I listened to some of the stories but you know, most of the time I turned the TV on. You just kind of have your own life at that time; your world is centered on you. I was a young mother, and having a little one running around didn't make grandma too happy. I kind of avoided them because my grandpa would talk and talk and talk. If I could turn back time, I wouldn't have just listened, I would have recorded. He talked about boat building all the time.

I knew I'd get to this point. I knew I'd get there to the point where I was ready to start learning and building and being active. But I wasn't then and I regret it to this day and for the rest of my life. I just hope that he would be proud of me now.

When I was younger, we had an IEA (Indian Education Act) teacher, name of Joe Kelly. He was really into Native arts for a while. He was white, from Louisiana. In his class we'd build miniatures. We also built games and we made fishhooks. I didn't understand how important it was then. It was just shop; it was fun. But now when I look back, those are probably some of the best memories I have. I even talked to Joe about starting a class or shop or something in Kodiak as recent as last year. I just didn't know how to go about it. I've always wanted to, but I never took that step. So even now I don't know if I could, but I'm getting there.

I would have to say it was amazing to be an apprentice on this boat. My ancestors were so much smarter than I could ever imagine. I had no idea the technology they had. I've always been proud to be Alutiiq, but recently I have come to having a new respect for my ancestors. I didn't know all the little things they had. I've learned they used grass for the inside of the seams when they sewed and just amazing things.[25]

On this boat, I carved. I did the bow piece and I did the thwarts, the pieces that run across. Eddie worked on those also. I think the cockpit coamings were done already. I did six out of the eight stringers. That was an interesting day; I got so tired of planing. I lashed and I stained. I've been a part of the entire process. I mean just because I'm quote, unquote "a girl" doesn't mean you're going to give me the sewing only to do. When Mike called me and asked me to be here, I said, "You know, you're not going to give me the girly chores. If so, I'm not going to do it."

There is an Alutiiq style of bow that is different from the Aleut one we worked on here. It comes up in two pieces, and it's a high bow style. That's my grandpa's style. Not all Alutiiq are high bowed. There are several different styles.

My grandmother has a picture on a postcard of my grandpa's kayak. She has it on loan to the Alutiiq Museum in Kodiak. She says, "There's no bow like grandpa's bow." So I let her know, I warned her ahead of time, that our bow wasn't the same style, so she wouldn't get mad at me when she came up. Also, for the Aleut, there are separate styles of bows.

I'm so grateful that Mike gave me the opportunity to be a part of this.

I sing to the seas
I sing to my kayak.
It is a part of my body,
we fly upon the waves.
It is my companion, my brother,
it is my wife.

If we die on the sea, we die together.
If we go down together, we remain together.
If I die an old man it will rest upon my grave,
and still we go on together.
And still we remain together.

Old Iñupiat song
Translation by David Hunsacker

Mike and Hope paddle their double-hatch kayak in Kachemak Bay at the
ceremony during which all of the boats went in the water for the first time.

Aleut Hunting Hats

June Simeonoff Pardue

Some of the Aleut hats were carved and some were steam bent. They were made out of driftwood. When you look at the underside of the hat, there is a ridge. They use that when they are out at sea. They would line up a spear with that. They would paint it black to keep down the glare. When you look at the outside, all the designs had a meaning. You could usually tell who was a whale hunter by the whale hunting design on the rim. It's a black and red zig-zag, teeth. The whale hunter's colors were black, red and white. Other people were sea otter hunters and you would see sea otter figures carved out of ivory put on the hat to look out at the ocean. I think they believed that the sea otter spirit would bring them to the sea otters. I saw one hat that had an eagle on it. People in our village were fond of eagles. They thought it was a mighty bird. It could fly so high. You could predict the weather by this bird. When bad weather was coming, it would fly really high.

June in her traditional beaded headdress.

People who hunted the birds would have the birds on their hats. If you look at the hats in museums, a lot of them will have silhouette art on them. It tells a story of a hunter's hunt. That would be on a more experienced hunter's hat. A young man would have just bands on his and a short visor. As they got older, they got longer visors. The chief in the village got the full crown. His hat was usually made by other hunters as a gift to him.

They had a chief hunter who would go out with them. They traveled for miles and miles. His job was to make sure they brought home enough food and to make sure the other hunters were safe. He had the sea lion whiskers with the beads in the back. If the wind began to get too rough, the beads would start to clack. That was his sign it was time to head back to shore.

All these men believed in the creator. They acknowledged the creator by painting designs on their hats. Men in our culture were spiritual leaders. That was their job. They were spiritual leaders of the household and spiritual leaders for the community. This belief is represented in the swirl pattern on the hats. You also see that on the bows or on the ivory volute that sticks out of the hat. It's put only on one side so it doesn't get in the way of him throwing his harpoon or spear. Today you see them on both sides because they are just doing it for decoration.

The hats also served the purpose of making them look like animals out on the sea. Sometimes they would use their hats like a mask. So when they were back in the village telling stories, they would flip their hat down and use that as part of the dance.

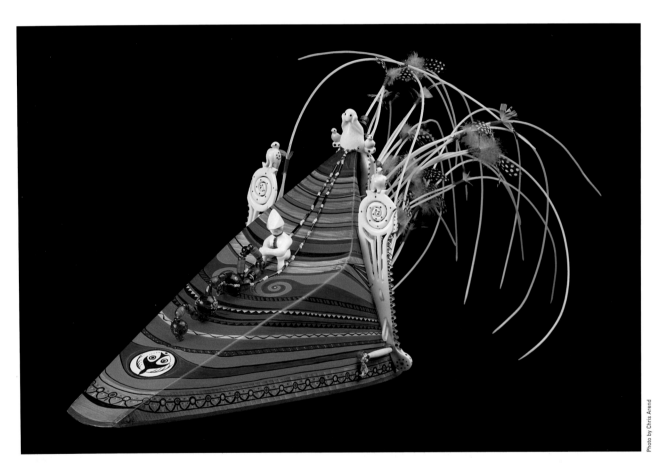

Bentwood Aleut hunting hat by Jacob Simeonoff in the
collection of Anchorage Museum of History and Art.

Alutiiq (Sugpiaq) Baidarka

Length: 3½ arm lengths   Width: 1 arm length   Depth: ½ arm length   Weight: 50 lbs.
Materials: Spruce and hardwood frame, sealskin covering.

Master boat builders: Nick Tanape Sr., Nanwalek, Alaska
Gregor Welpton, Juneau, Alaska
Apprentices: Nick Tanape Jr., Kilann Moonin, Jeremy Cook
Skin sewers: Grace Harrod, June Simeonoff Pardue, Nick Tanape, Gregor Welpton

A distinguishing feature of the Alutiiq boats is the upswept bifid or forked bow, much more accentuated in form than the Aleut. The lower part serves as a cutwater and the upper flotation piece assists with maneuverability under difficult conditions. Nick Tanape comments on this:

It helps when you're out there in the rough water. It definitely works. I don't know whose idea it was, but you would have to be very smart to figure that out. They traveled in very rough seas out here. I've been in a boat where a forty- or fifty-foot boat couldn't travel where our people traveled in their fifteen- to sixteen-foot kayaks.

They landed on the rocks on the beach with no problem. The bigger boats would just sink.

Finding a skin sewer that had experience with the waterproof stitch and working sealskins became a difficult task for the Alutiiq and Aleut groups. Finally, Grace Harrod, who is originally from Mekoryuk on Nunivak Island but lives in Kodiak today, was found. She had never worked with sealskin but had become quite proficient with the waterproof stitch while working on deer hide. Both crews were very happy to find her. She trained other women and men so the skill will be more readily available on future projects.

Nick Tanape Sr. sews skin for his Alutiiq kayak.

NICK TANAPE SR.

I was born 1946, in Nanwalek. That was called English Bay before and they changed it back to Nanwalek. I grew up over in that area there during the time that kayaking was at the tail end.

I guess my dad, Joe Tanape, did a lot of traveling in those kayaks. His Alutiiq name was Jun. He was born somewhere around Seward. He talked a lot about the Seward area. I heard a lot of stories about the kayaking from him. They traveled all the way around Seward and into Kodiak, all the way around Kachemak Bay area. When he was very little he used to tell the story that he'd run away from home, from his parents, and hide in his grandfather's kayak. He'd crawl inside the bow and by the time they were so many miles away, they find him and it's too late for them to return.

I'd been working with the Pratt Museum in Homer and I started getting interested in kayaking. Then six years ago, I started as an apprentice with Gregor Welpton. We had funding to go ahead to build some baidarkas with the school kids. I wanted to teach the kids what I've known and what I heard, and tell them more about the stories from the past. We wrote some books and CD ROMs about all this.

Technology
Gregor and I built three traditional frames. We used airplane fabric to cover them. Seal is not available like it used to be. The fabric lasts for a long time like twenty, thirty years; sealskins probably last only a year or two. You got to replace them. They've got to have special care; take them off the kayaks every year and store them away in cool, dry place if you can; keep them from getting spoiled.

The frames are good for a long time too if there is special care taken with them. If one of the ribs broke, they'd always have pieces ready. It takes a long time to gather all the material they need from the beaches – years.

For this baidarka the keelson is spruce. The hoop on top is hardwood, oak. The gunwales are spruce. We had to buy lumber. At home we have spruce trees but they are small and knotty. What they did a long time ago is waited and looked around on the beaches for a nice straight piece of spruce with no knots in it, and then they took it home and started splitting it. It took them a long time to do that kind of gathering there; it didn't happen like in a year. It took a couple of years to gather all that stuff. When they were out hunting, they'd find a nice piece of wood that they could use and they'd take that home and start cutting it up and save it for the next kayak. They had to know how the grain went and follow it. They had all the names for all kinds of wood and I'm not familiar with that too much. I'm just learning now too, how to name these things. I work with curriculum in the school. It's a new writing system with Alutiiq language.

I couldn't get enough sealskin from home because we are losing a lot of our seals. They are declining by six percent a year. I belong to the Harbor Seal Commission and I work with them trying to figure out what's causing it. It's getting costly now to buy the sealskin from the other villages. We have to buy from up north. The ones we used here were about a hundred dollars a skin. They are de-haired and dried up by the sun.

We treat our skins with seal oil to keep them waterproof. You use moss and seal oil, mix them together to fill the little cracks or holes in the sewing. Or you can use something else like tree pitch to do that. Whichever is available, that's what they'll use.

No nails or no screws or glue were used on this boat at all. We couldn't get the real sinew. It was costly, so the closest we could get is the imitation sinew for lashing. Everything is lashed together. We put a deck design of a seal for me. The sea otter was for my partner, Gregor. That went on the inside on a block in the cockpit.

In case they punctured their baidarka, they always carried a little pouch with needles and thread. They always had to carry sinew for thread. Whenever they hunt, they saved all the sinew they could. Sinew was from any type of animal they could get, like in our area maybe from moose or bear. It wasn't always available.

Apprentices
We decided to bring back the apprentices we used six years ago when we did another baidarka for the Park Service. They are more experienced now and a little quicker and they know what they're doing now. We brought three of them. One of them was my son. He's twenty-one. He stayed with it during the time we built the frame and we had another kid, Nathan. He's getting to be like an expert now. And we used another lady; she's good at building frames.

Traditional Roles
We talked about traditional roles before we did the skin with Grace Harrod and June Pardue. We didn't have enough men and ladies to do all that. We talked about it. Traditionally, it was spoken awhile back (now people don't believe in those stories) that the women couldn't go over the canoe or kayak; gives them bad luck. Women's hair stuck in the sewing there; men had to watch it very carefully. That would be bad luck.

Now they say, "Oh we can bring some ladies into doing all kinds of things." So we all agreed, it's time. The men do the sewing now too.

The Future
This is going to carry on and I'm gonna do some more when I go home. I'm learning a lot too. I've been visiting with the Yup'ik group. I can understand pretty much what they're saying and talking about. They start

Gregor Welpton's wood working tools.

understanding me real well too. By watching what they are doing, that's another language. We don't have to know the words to understand. They are the same techniques, like sewing and putting the lashing together and all that goes with it. It's similar work. They must have had to travel to look at other people's work too and it's really neat.

This is the best project I've ever seen. It makes me think like the old ways and it just gives me the feeling that I've been there. Sometimes it's heartbreaking just knowing it. Like I say, I must've been here before and I've done it before. It just comes to you.

GREGOR WELPTON

I'm thirty-five years old and I've been building kayaks for seventeen years. I built my first one when I was seventeen years old. There are boat builders in my family.

I was born outside of Boston. My ancestry is all-American. There's a bunch of Irish, Welsh, Scots, a real mixture. I came up to Alaska when I was about fifteen years old. I participated in commercial fishing. I'm a journeyman shipwright. I re-built boats for a living. The kayaks are a personal passion of mine. I really think that seeing this knowledge through, and successfully seeing it in the hands of the younger generation, is probably one of the most important things. I kind of stumbled into it backwards.

In working with Nick on this project, it has really been the continuation of the work that I've done with the students at Nanwalek. I went into Nanwalek twice and we built three boats down there in the village. That's how I met Nick.

I left Alaska and went down to college in Olympia, Washington, at Evergreen State College. I had been studying all kinds of crazy subjects. I was deeply involved in energy systems and energy systems research. We were looking at hydroelectric plants and all the kinds of solar cells and methane gas digesters and things like this. In the midst of the program I was taking, Reagan got into office and destroyed the "Energy 2000" report and the budget and everything that I was really working on a personal level. Where there had been a future and jobs and things like that we could do, suddenly that whole thing was just no longer there. He basically said, "No, let's get Detroit rolling again and let's pump as much fuel as we can pump." So, I was pretty depressed at that point.

I've always loved spending time on the water, and I ended up borrowing a friend's kayak and canoe and that's how I got back and forth to school every morning. I used to paddle across the inlet and hike up through the woods there on the backside of the campus.

The kayak, for me, was sort of like a solace. I was pretty depressed at that point. I felt like the things that I really believed in, that I'd been working on, were just so easily shattered by the whims of just a few select powerful people. That was kind of a rough thing at age seventeen.

So I just kind of dug a little deeper and I started looking for other things. It was about that time I ran into a friend of mine, Joseph Waterhouse, and Joseph kind of took me under his wing and said, "Look, I see something in you and I don't know what it is." We just became friends over time. It turned out that Joseph was busy putting plans together to build great voyaging canoes from the Suquamish area and tie back in with the Maori who, at the time, were building voyaging canoes coming up out of the South Pacific. He'd been adopted into a clan down there and they were talking and trading and all this other stuff. This was prior to "Paddle to Seattle."[26]

Paddle to Seattle

We built a boat for "Paddle to Seattle." I worked with David Forlines and all of those guys down at La Push. My mentor and my teacher, Joseph, he was a man of great vision, along with David, and the two of them recognized that in each other. They both really drew out the best in each other. I would go with Joseph just to help with the canoes.

When they built the first canoes at La Push, nobody had any memory of what they were trying to do at all. These were the first canoes that were going to hit the Pacific Ocean in a hundred twenty years from La Push. At that point, we were looking at traditional knowledge that had all but been forgotten. Trying to resurrect it was just an ominous task.

I helped shaping, doing a lot of the adz work and stuff like that on the canoe. I was there when we steamed her open. Then I was there for the launching as well. The launching was a disaster. The canoe rolled over. It was a rough day. People didn't know how to handle a boat that big. They went broadside to the waves and went right over. It wasn't very encouraging, especially because this was one of the first boats being completed in the area within the three-year period prior to the "Paddle to Seattle," the bicentennial celebration. Everybody was looking to La Push for inspiration back then.

So, that was an interesting time and we all had to rally inside ourselves and say, "Look we all have a lot to learn and we should keep on going." That was really an important lesson then. I've gotten lots of different, very important lessons through this whole thing. There are times to just keep pushing, and there are times to step back and say, "Okay, I'm just going to stop here."

So I worked with Joe and Joe passed me off to one of his cousins, the Makah, Greg Colfax. I then sort of tutored and learned under Greg. I told Joseph that all of this time I'd been dreaming and wanting to build kayaks.

Previous page: Gregor Welpton lashes member of frame for Alutiiq kayak.
Above: Gregor sights along the kayak keelson.

The canoe and participating in the canoe culture was a very powerful thing and it drew me in. It gave me a warmth of people around me and things, but I really liked the quiet solo water travel that you get in a kayak.

In order to take to the water, I really felt like I needed to build my own kayak. I was seventeen. I told Greg what I was thinking about doing. At that time, I just wanted to paddle right back up to Alaska. That's pretty much all I was looking for.

Greg said, "Okay, I'm going to send you on a journey." That was pretty much the only way he knew how to deal with me. It was like he said, "You're doing something that I don't really know how to do, but I'm willing to help guide you through it." He taught me how to carve. He sent me on a journey to gather all the things I was going to need. I needed to gather knowledge, materials; I needed to gather tools. All these different parts were part of the whole beginning of the kayak-building process. He sent me off to another Greg, Greg Blomberg on Lopez Island, who taught me the intricacies of tool building, knife making, and making carving tools. When I was on Lopez Island, I met Chris Cunningham who is now the editor of *Sea Kayaker* magazine and Chris showed me how to build these mainland kayaks that he'd been teaching for close to twenty years. It was an interesting journey. Then he sent me up to this other Greg up in Port Townsend. It was just Greg, Greg and Greg.

I gathered my tools up and I started building this boat. It took me probably about a year and a half to build my first kayak. Greg's dad, Lloyd Colfax, was on staff at Evergreen College at the time and he put me in his Native American Studies program. They got permission for me to go down to the Lowie Museum in Berkeley and I got into the archives down there. I got to sit back there with all the kayaks. This was back in 1983 or '84.

The guy basically made me wear little gloves and sat me back there and I took notes on all of the joinery techniques, all the lashing techniques. I just sat and sketched. I filled sketchbooks with of all of this stuff back then. I just drew everything that I could and wrote all kinds of notes. They were really helpful. Those notes became the foundation cornerstone of what I was doing.

Later on David Zimmerly published his papers and George Dyson finally published his book. It all started coming together after this first boat. I didn't even know George Dyson when I was building this boat and somebody kept saying, "You got to read this book. You got to read this book. This guy built this boat just like you. Read *Starship and the Canoe*."[27]

The next thing I know, I'm taking a trip up to Vancouver to go find George and learn what I can from him. He and I corresponded a lot.

One of the biggest mistakes people make when they're trying to build a kayak is they go and look at the widest collection of all of the different types of frames on record and all of their lines. A lot of people try to build their kayaks from those lines. Those lines are not correct. Those lines came from boats that had been stored on their sides or hung in museums. All the frames are distorted. They do not show the real shape. I found this out after about my second boat. It's due to damage from the storage conditions. There's just no way you can get around that with a skin boat. They are fragile creatures, period. I'm sure nobody in the museums would like to hear me say that, but that's really the case.

Being in a kayak is great solitude. It's some of the best solitude on earth. The only other time that I feel that good – but it's a totally different thing – is like when I'm out hunting mountain goats and I'm up

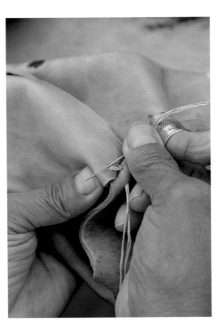

The important waterproof stitch that all of the skin sewers either knew or were learning consists of a blind stitch on what is to be the outside of the skin and a reinforcing whipstitch on the inside.

walking the ridges by myself on the snow line. Being on the water is just that, that sense of yourself on this planet. You're slipping into the planet itself. The wonderful thing is that you're slipping into an animal itself. You get to take your own animal form that way. You get out and there you are, your own animal, and back in the other reality – not the reality of day-to-day roads and steel and asphalt and all this other crap that's going on – but you know you are just in it.

At this point in my building career I use no plans, no measurement, no anything. I pick up the wood and... in fact, I won't even pick up the wood if the wood isn't speaking to me beforehand. But once the piece of wood that I've got starts speaking, I decide to make it sing, and the board, the woods, the tools, all of this kind of comes together. What might look like a chaotic flow from the outside really becomes one great big song to me of creation. And that's why I build these things, because I hear it in my head, I feel it through my heart, it comes out through my hands and the boat is just completely born.

If you asked me what is the size of these, I couldn't even tell you. I don't know. I've forgotten all of that stuff. I don't work that way. I do it all by eye. I do everything by a feeling, it's not just eyeing. I can tell if I can feel it inside of me and everything's good, then I know it's a go. If something's off just a little, I'll be sitting there saying, "No, that's not right." It just kind of makes me a little queasy in my stomach until it's all just there. That's what it's all about.

The Project

This boat is a real interesting boat for me. I got the paperwork and I looked at it and I realized that this wasn't a venue for me. This was really a showcase of Native artists doing their own art, and at that point I decided I wasn't even going to apply. I said, "I'm not interested because I don't want to take the light away from anybody else who would do this."

Then they called me back up and said they had just been on the phone with Nick Tanape, and he would only do this project if I would do it with him. I said, "Okay, I'll call Nick." So, I called up Nick and I said, "Why'd you want to drag me into this thing?" And he said, "Oh come on, it'll be fun. The two of us can do this and it'll be a real good chance for me to continue working with you."

Nick and I came up in early May. Summertime is not typically the boat building time of year. Historically people built boats in the wintertime. When you think about our lifestyles here in this state, you know we'd rather be hunting, fishing, out on the water, using this time of year for what gets us out of the house. With this boat building in the summer, I've recognized there's a lot of challenges trying to keep the materials cool, trying not to get your wood to shatter and bust open because of the light.

The highest point of the whole thing for me is bringing all of these people together for us to share and to see inside each other's lives. We get to see inside each other's techniques and to show what those variations of techniques bring out.

Carving the frame for the bifid bow. This gets covered with skin, retaining the two-part configuration. The bottom part serves as a cutwater and the top, a flotation aid.

I feel really privileged to be working with the people that I'm working with here, and to be a part of this thing, and learn from all the other builders around me. Being here with Grace and June is a lot the same, learning the skin work and stuff like that.

I'm pretty nimble with my fingers and I know a lot about stitching. My mom taught me to sew when I was about four years old and I've always loved sewing. She taught me how to needlepoint too. I remember one time, I was going to camp. I was about seven years old, and all the other guys were like, "What is with you? What are you doing?" I was sitting around doing needlepoint. Up to that point, I didn't even realize there was anything that was wrong about it.

So the sewing is real natural; I just needed to learn the stitch. I've never had to sew for waterproofness prior to this because we've always used artificial means of waterproofing. I built a couple of kayaks for museums where we've tried to make the artificial skins look as though they were sealskins. It's a mixture of beeswax and straight paraffin. You get the coloration of the beeswax in it.

The Meaning of Tradition

We've been asked by the Alaska Native Heritage Center to keep this boat entirely traditional. I've always lashed entirely the traditional way and I've always pegged everything as true to form as possible. I don't use sinew to lash my kayaks together because it would take sinew from too many animals to lash a kayak. I feel like that's a waste, especially when you can get an artificial substitute. So we had this big question:"What is traditional?"

I mean, is traditional something that's happened prior to 1950? Or is traditional an ever-evolving thing that we all are participating in which enables us to get our work done as properly and as efficiently as possible? The first guy who discovered an electric drill was, of course, going to use that rather than a hand drill. So, there's been a lot of this with the tradition.

The Future

I see a lot of different futures and a lot of it is so much centered on media and how the media perceives this and how they take it and run with it. We're living in one of the most interesting times where we can get streaming digital video out to a village that otherwise has very limited resources. This is a time when we can take a sort of post-production video of this and we can stream it into a lot of the schools and they can get a real hands-on good visual course in how to do this kind of thing.

I used to have a dream. About eight years ago, I thought that if we managed to teach at least the frame building – because the frame building I feel is my specialty – we teach this in the villages and set up a sporting event a lot like the Eskimo Olympics but water-based. These are a water-based people. The neatest thing in the world to do would be all of the exercises and all of the old events they used to do that were based around the kayak. Nick has begun with the gathering of kayaks and stuff like that down in Homer. What I had imagined was getting each of the schools to field a team of kids to be trained in rolling, in paddling backwards, and in paddling under water upside-down – all kinds of different competitions and stuff. If there's a competitive element to it, it gives people even more reason to do the training and to get themselves out there.

JUNE SIMEONOFF PARDUE

My Alutiiq name is Aatcha. I was born at Old Harbor on Kodiak Island and grew up there until the 1964 earthquake and tsunami. In our younger years, we traveled back and forth between Old Harbor and Kuguiak. The village no longer exists.

We didn't have a school like we do today. I have relatives in my family who contributed to my knowledge. They taught us the old way, all the elders passing the information along to the young people. They trained us to respect elders, to know what the chain of authority is, taught us our roles, especially the girls. As a young girl I used to think in order to be a good Alutiiq woman, I had to learn how to weave baskets. I admired my mother, so at a young age I was picking up her scrap grass off the floor and she and her teacher, Fedosha Inga, saw that. So they moved me from the floor to the table with them. So I wove my first basket when I was twelve.

I remember us getting ready for the evening, hearing the stories of how the men used to hunt and how the women helped prepare the men for hunting. The stories would go on late into the night. Half the time we fell asleep on our mother's lap. Some of the stories they told were how they used to sea otter hunt. They even had a song about that, how they would circle around the sea otters in their kayaks and beat their paddles into the ocean until the sea otter got tired. It would come up for air and that's when they went in for the kill.

I credit my father, the late Jacob James Simeonoff Sr., for sharing so many things with me in his last days. He died of cancer and spent his last days with me. We stayed up talking at my dining table for hours until he was too tired. Fortunately it was just him and me and my two daughters, who were little children at the time. He told me stories and some very personal things about our family.

My dad used to tell me when the men would go out hunting, they were very quiet. They would go out in the kayaks and they would put their paddle in the ocean and they would put the handle in their mouth and hold it between their teeth. If there is movement under there, something swimming around, they could tell. That's their sonar.

Working on this kayak has been a really good experience. We work well together. It's like it was meant to be. It was already planned a long time ago for us to be together. That is what we call "predestined." The skin sewing, it's a real learning experience for me. I'm just so grateful to Nick for inviting me to be a part of this, and for Gregor also and for Grace showing me the waterproof stitch. Working with the sealskins, to me it's an honor. I don't ever remember a time in any of the villages I lived in when they did that, not in my lifetime.

The men used to be the ones who would sew their own boats because then their life was in their own hands. Like with Nikka (Tanape), he wants to have the best people skin sewing for him, especially if it's going to be a boat that he will take out in the ocean. I really keep that in mind because they are putting their lives in our hands.

This project is wonderful. It's the first time in history and I hope it continues. This is a birthing of cultural events taking place.

I'm pretty excited about getting to work with the Aleut boat too.

GRACE HARROD

I'm from Nunivak Island from the village of Mekoryuk. I live in the city of Kodiak now. I was born June 14, 1938. My Cup'ik name is Nussan. It was my grandma's name. I'm carrying it. My present mother, Mary Smith, taught me. My mom died when I was three years old, but dad got remarried and she taught me. As she was sewing, I watched her a lot.

My experience with skin sewing was I started with mukluks. But this is the very first time I ever sewed sealskin on a kayak frame. It's kind of rough on your hands. When I was a little girl, I used to come home from school and I'd see all these women in my mama's kitchen, my aunts and my grandmas there sewing. I told myself then, when I grow up, I'm not ever going to sew a kayak. But so far, I have been asked to sew about five deerskin hide kayaks, baidarki. Deer hide is very easy; it absorbs water very easily. You soak it ten to fifteen minutes; it's ready to be sewn. But with sealskin, it's very time consuming.

Because we know the skin will shrink after we put it on the frame, we just approximate it, maybe an inch and a half shrinkage. When it shrinks it might break the ribs. So we just give it a lot of room.

My mom taught me this waterproof stitch. Most of the Natives use it. We are all learning here as this is the very first time with sealskin. June and I were familiar with using our hands, so I am fortunate to have her helping us.

These guys, they are very neat to work with. They are down-to-earth, my kind of people. They are really fun to work with. When everyone gets too serious, I have to tell them a joke. We always end up laughing; we are a happy people. Natives are a happy people anyway. We laugh a lot. We just laugh at little things and we talk in our dialect and if you say it in our dialect, Cup'ik, it's very funny to other people. I speak in Cup'ik and they speak in Alutiiq but we can understand each other.

I called my mom on the phone in Mekoryuk. I said, "Mom, I'm going to sew a kayak." Over the phone she just hollered, "You don't know how." So, my dad, Peter Smith, got on the phone and I said, "Dad, I'm going to sew a kayak." He said, "It's going to sink" in Eskimo. He started laughing. I said "Dad, its going to be in a museum. They're going to put it in a museum when I'm done with it." He said, "Go ahead, sew it. It won't sink in a museum."

He has passed on now. I know he's here watching me now on this kayak with a big smile on his face; I can see him smiling a block away!

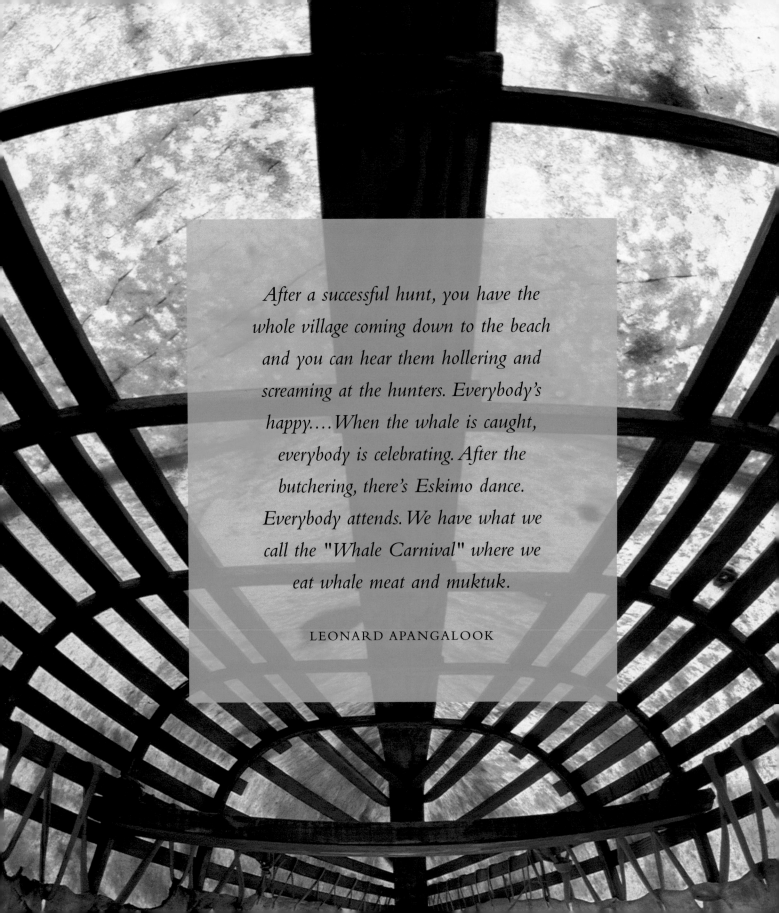

After a successful hunt, you have the whole village coming down to the beach and you can hear them hollering and screaming at the hunters. Everybody's happy....When the whale is caught, everybody is celebrating. After the butchering, there's Eskimo dance. Everybody attends. We have what we call the "Whale Carnival" where we eat whale meat and muktuk.

LEONARD APANGALOOK

Open Skin Boats

Skin boats in general have a very old history, possibly beginning in the first millennium B.C. in Europe.[28] They were comparatively easy boats to build, requiring simple tools, a frame made from available wood, and the skins of local animals.

The builders of open skin boats in Alaska and Siberia lived in treeless habitats for the most part, the coasts of the Arctic Ocean and the Bering Sea. They had access to large amounts of driftwood washed out from local drainages. Also readily available were tough marine mammal skins for coverings. With these factors taken into consideration, this type of boat could naturally evolve. This craft provided a seaworthy means of transportation for hunting, travel and carrying cargo in rough seas.

Roger S. Silook, elder from St. Lawrence Island, relates what he heard from old-timers from his region in his book, *Seevookuk*:

Before the white people came, St. Lawrence Island was called Seevookuk which means "squeezed." The island was shaped like a piece of blubber they had squeezed to drain out the oil. Gambell was called Seevookuk too, after the whole island, as it is the oldest village. They did not have any map like we do now but they find out the shape by traveling around the island using the sun and stars as compass. In good clear days, the best compass they used was the wind and the condition of the waves and current. They determine which way the current was moving by putting down a line with a sinker on the end.

In those days the boats they use were flat bottom and almost upright sides. These used no nails but lashed together the whole framework. Mostly baleen was used to lash the ribs and bottom of boat.... The biggest boats they have was about twenty-five feet long and five to six feet wide. They do not use foot measurement because they use fathom. No matter how tall or short a man is, his fathom is his measurement. The boat can carry twenty-five to thirty people or about five tons of cargo.[29]

Today the St. Lawrence Island *angyapiks* and the Iñupiat umiaks are still actively made as whaling boats which attests to their great versatility over time. Leonard Apangalook indicates in his narrative that this is also partly due to the Alaska Eskimo Whaling Commission's rules, which mandates their use in the hunt.[30]

The design of the St. Lawrence Island *angyapik* has evolved over time. Before the 1930s, these boats had flat bottoms and their frames were constructed out of driftwood. Today they have a rounded bottom on the hull and the frames are made out of commercially milled hardwood such as hickory and oak. The boat builders also added an exterior, or false, keel made of ironwood or ivory which, combined with the rounded bottom, makes the job of moving the boat over the ice much easier.[31] It saves on wear and tear to the skin coverings as they aren't exposed to the abrasive surfaces of the ice. In addition, metal nails, marine paints and commercial sealants are used in the construction process. Walrus skins are still used for the coverings, but the addition of commercial sealants and paints adds longevity to them.

Umiak or open skin boat used as a temporary shelter, Nome, Alaska.

Traveling by skin boat, St. Michael, Alaska.

Siberian Yupik (Bering Straits Yupik) — Angyapik

Length: 20′ 8″   Width: 5′   Depth: 30″   Weight: 500 lbs.
Materials: hickory and fir wood frame, 2 walrus hides split, seal skin rope for lashing,
silicone and oil-based sealant

Master boat builders: Leonard Apangalook Sr., Gambell, Alaska
Ronald Apangalook, Wasilla, Alaska
Apprentices: Justus Apangalook, John Apangalook
Skin sewers: Susan Campbell, Mildred Apangalook, Carolyn Apangalook
Darlene Rexford, Barbara Apangalook

This whaling boat was the only boat in the project that is still actively made and used for subsistence in its original form. Two whalers, father and son, were the leads for the construction and it was obvious, by the speed with which they worked, building a skin boat was like second nature to them. The walrus hides for the covering and sealskins for the rope were harvested and prepared on St. Lawrence Island and shipped to the construction site. The walrus hides were placed on frames and expertly split in half during early spring. This process gives double the amount of coverage from one hide. Journal entries show these men to be efficient hunters also:

May 13 – Ron arrived Gambell from Wasilla to help harvest hides for the boat.

May 15 – Harvested two walrus hides in a day-long hunt.

May 22 – Harvested two bearded seal for hide rope (lashing).

When the boat was finished, the crew built a boat rack and placed the angyapik upside-down on the rack, which is the traditional method to store both these boats and also the Iñupiat umiaks.

LEONARD APANGALOOK SR.

I come from Gambell on St. Lawrence Island. My Eskimo name is Piitkuk. It means "One that grew like a plant." That's the meaning of my name. I have lived out at Gambell for sixty-one years. I went to school

Leonard Apangalook Sr. and his grandson.

Outside, but most of my life I have spent out there in Gambell. I ran the local store for twenty-six years, then retired. I was also magistrate up there for seventeen years. I retired early from the state also.

Angyapik is the word for our boat. It's different from the mainlanders because we speak Siberian Yupik. This is the third boat I have built. I enjoy working with these boats. One of the things I went to school for was cabinet making and millwork which has to do with wood. So building the frame out of wood has been a lot of fun.

The Construction Process

The only driftwood we have on this boat is the front, the bow that curves. The rest, we bought commercially from a lumberyard.

Traditionally, the frame would be all driftwood. We do get a lot of driftwood on the island, probably from Russia since we are only thirty-eight miles from there. There are some major rivers across there that wash out a lot of timber and we do get a lot of it. It would be basically fir and cedar we would use on the boat.

It took us two and a half weeks to build it. We soaked the hides for five days in the water before we draped them over the frame. Once we begin that process of lashing it on, it's just a one-day job. The women do the sewing. We (men and women) both split the walrus hides. We do that pretty early in June and late May, split the hides and dry them.

This boat is exclusively for whaling. We actually sail the boat when we pursue the whale. The mainlanders paddle their umiaks. We sail when we go after the whale. It has to be the most exotic way of hunting a whale. Sometimes I have so much fun sailing, I have to remind myself I'm supposed to be whaling.

Today the sail is made out of canvas. I imagine before, it would have been walrus gut or seal skin. With a good wind you can move along pretty good. With the higher winds, a maximum speed of wind that we can tolerate with this boat would probably be fifteen knots.

Above and right: Apprentices fit
stringers for traditional angyapik frame.

Sometimes it has gone up to twenty, twenty-five knot winds and that's been a little like motoring along with a twenty-five-horse outboard motor.

The sail is rectangular shaped. By comparison to modern sailing boats, it's kind of a stout sail. On my particular boat, I have a twenty-one-foot mast and the boom on the bottom is about the same length. We can lower it up or down. We have reefers on there, so with a higher wind we can reduce the size of the sail. The mast is placed about one quarter of the way back from the bow.

Boston Whaler

This particular model that we built here was designed after the Boston Whaler. In the mid-1800s, when the commercial whalers went up the Bering Straits, they brought with them the Boston Whaler, a wooden boat. They traded with our people for baleen and provided some of these whaling boats, but they were so heavy, being made out of wood. So our people designed this hide boat, this walrus-skin boat,

after that Boston Whaler. We put a frame together that was very strong structurally and then covered it with walrus hide.

Prior to this era, we also had a boat covered with walrus hide and if I were to make one of those, it would be identical to the ones we have up north on the mainland like at Point Barrow and Point Hope. So this style we use now does have history which, as I explained, was influenced by the commercial whalers prior to the 1900s.

Whaling

We have a fleet of twenty-four boats who are members of the local whaling association. They are registered with the Alaska Eskimo Whaling Commission. We can strike eight or lance six, which ever comes first, for our village. We hunt the bowheads.

We're mandated by the International Whaling Commission to use our traditional harpoons. There is a bomb attached to the harpoon gun. This tool was designed in the late 1800s by the commercial whalers and of course, we started using that too. There's a harpoon iron with a line attached to it with a couple of floats attached to the line. The gun, itself, sits on top of the harpoon. When you strike a whale, the harpoon is attached along with the line and floats. The gun injects into the whale a time-delayed bomb and the bomb explodes inside the whale. Normally, with a good shot, it's an instant kill after the initial strike.

Today, we use outboard motors to tow the whale into the village. Once the whale is struck, all the other boats converge on the successful hunter and they take part in the kill, towing it into the village. Like I said, we have about twenty-four crews that whale, and we all tie onto the whale and tow it into the village.

The captain of the successful boat designates. He forms somewhat of a committee to handle the butchering and the dividing, making sure everybody gets a share. It's a communal activity.

Under the Marine Mammal Protection Act, we're mandated to utilize all of the animal that we can. I used to be vice-chairman of the Alaska Eskimo Whaling

Commission. We got to travel around quite a bit, meeting with the International Whaling Commission. I've been to Iceland, Scotland, England, Japan and Russia. We're supported by Greenpeace and Friends of the Animals because we do it traditionally and for subsistence. We don't do any commercial whaling like Japan and Norway did at one time. They imposed a moratorium on those two a few years back because they were doing it more or less commercially.

So, we have in support of our whaling activity some very big organizations in the world, some of these special interest groups. Plus the fact we've employed the best scientists to study the bowhead since 1971. We recruit the nation's best-qualified marine biologists to help us at these international meetings. Our country is very much respected by the rest of the world because, I'm very proud to say, we are very ably represented by our government, our scientists and our leaders. It's a good feeling.

A young hand silhouettes through the outer skin of traditional angyapik during launching ceremony at Homer. Right: The finished angyapik.

Traditionally they had ceremonies at whaling time, but that was before my time. I have read about them and seen some movies of them, but we don't practice any of these ceremonies anymore.

The Future
We are a very small community. The whole village and the young people work together in the hunts. We're still training our young people how to whale, how to respect the animals and that's perpetual from a long time back. It still continues today.

We're passing the boat building on too. Working with me here, I had my two sons; one is twelve years old, and my two nephews are under twenty. We're very strong subsistence users still.

I'm really glad that a boat design by the St. Lawrence Islanders was desired by the Heritage Center and that this boat will be able to represent our island. It is my hope that it will make a lot of people happy that come here. I always enjoy looking at a boat like this.

RONALD APANGALOOK

My Yupik name is Qaygeghutkaq. I'm thirty-one years old. I was raised in Gambell, Sivuqaq. I now live in Wasilla. I'm a full-time artist. I do my Native material, materials like whalebone and ivory. I also do stone. I'm moving into the harder stone now, like alabaster and marble. I've been carving for nine years now.

My inspiration is Siberian Yupik. But some of it comes from Alan Houser. I know one of his students, from the Institute of American Indian Art in Santa Fe, New Mexico, Larry Ahvakana.

My dad and I, Leonard, were the master boat builders. I learned a lot of my boat building from Mr. Oozeva when I was in high school. We built three boats. I also built one boat with my dad, so we kind of mixed our knowledge. This is my fifth boat.

I think our apprentices learned a lot on this project. They learned about the certain angles. For instance, how you line the center of the boat with the bow and the stern, then you build around that. You start with the bow, you shape it and then you attach the keel. I think

they really learned that if you can get those three pieces – the bow, the stern and the keel – that's the hardest part. Then the ribs just come.

After we put the keel, stern and bow together, we leveled it on the ground and then we put our gunwales on. We found the center of the boat and then we started the steaming and installation of the ribs. We installed the seats, stained the frame, sewed the hides together and lashed them onto the frame. After the skins were in place, we put the silicone and sealant on them.

Whaling

I started whaling when I was seven years old with my grandfather. My dad was the striker at the time. In 1979, my dad became a captain. When I was eighteen I struck a whale. I was the striker for my dad's crew.

We have a lot of wind out in our area. Rather than paddling, we utilize the wind. We usually go out when it's between ten and twenty knots. There are four different sizes for our sail. We can reduce the size of the sail down if the wind picks up out there.

We have a rudder, and on the boat we built here, we have four seats. For this boat, there would be a crew of five to six.

After a successful hunt, you have the whole village coming down to the beach and you can hear them hollering and screaming at the hunters. Everybody's happy. I do remember a time when the quota system was first put into place. You were allowed three strikes, three landed. We lost all three whales that year. Normally, the hunters come back in the evening. But after the third strike was lost, all of the hunters came home early and rather than being happy, everybody was crying. It was really sad. When the whale is caught, everybody is celebrating. After the butchering, there's Eskimo dance. Everybody attends. We have what we call the "Whale Carnival" where we eat whale meat and muktuk.[32]

The Future

I would like to see more guys my age, and the younger people going to the high school now, building boats and sleds just so we can continue this and teach our children and their children. One of the things we have lost is the kayak building. Even among the elders in Gambell today, there might be one or two that still knows how to do it, but they are too old to share that with us. If we could get more guys building boats and sleds and other hunting equipment, I think we'll be able to pass that on. It's kind of scary when the language is starting to go; you start to wonder when some of the skills will start to go. I'd also like to see more young women learning how to sew. My wife is a year younger than I am. She's sewn on two boats now and she still can't remember how to do the stitches. She has to be taught again each time. I'd like to see a boat building class.

I started this because I love to hunt. It saddens me to see some communities using the skiffs for their walrus hunting and, even in Gambell we use the skiffs, but this boat here, this skin boat, we use for whaling. I start to wonder how much longer we will be using these boats.

It was really good to work with my dad. We've been on one other boat project that was a little different than this, because we used fiberglass for the covering. You continue to learn, even if you're familiar with the whole thing. I always seem to learn a little more with each building of a boat. So, that was really nice. I learned a lot from my dad, and hopefully, in twenty years, I can build a boat with my son.

The angyapik paddled by a crew in waters off Homer.

*I hope that what I'm doing, and
the documentation that's being done
on the Against the Wind, can be
my way of expressing the need for
keeping this alive, keep it going.
It's such an important part of our
history, our tradition, that it
should not be lost.*

WAYNE PRICE

Dugout Canoes

Mist combs the rainforest daily in southeast Alaska. The climate encourages the growth of large cedar trees. For this region's first people – the Tlingit, Haida, Tsimshian and Eyak – these majestic beings of the forest were treated with great respect. From their bark and wood came clothing, containers, mats, totem poles, house posts, screens and canoes.

The Northwest Coast cultures held their canoes in great esteem for they were one of the most important subsistence items a village, clan or a family could possess. Living in a landscape that is governed by the tides, wind and ocean currents demands a mode of transportation that is seaworthy for travel and for gathering the rich marine resources.

The people of this land used spruce, cottonwood (for river travel) and most importantly, when available, western red cedar to build their canoes. However the western red cedar trees grow only in the southern part of Southeast Alaska. The more northerly communities had to obtain this coveted material as driftwood or in trade.

The most desired canoes were the high-prowed, red cedar craft made by the Haidas, who lived further south in the Queen Charlotte Islands. These large ocean-going vessels termed the "northern style" or "broad nose," *Lukadawóox'* in Tlingit, allowed the people of Southeast to travel great distances carrying many passengers and cargo.

Our people traveled up and down the coast in those big canoes. Our people had a name for the polar bear, heentak xóodzi; underwater brown bear, x'ada s'aak, the walrus. The only way they could have named these things is that they traveled up there. There are stories about traveling up to the Arctic and down the coast down to South America. Our history is full of these stories.
— Paul Jackson Sr., Tlingit elder [33]

An earlier style of vessel called the head canoe existed in the late-eighteenth century. According to Holm this was probably the principal canoe used in the early historic period among the people of the Northwest Coast. [34] Its use presumably extended from Vancouver Island to Yakutat. The head canoe is characterized by a heavy, almost vertical bowfin, a stern with more flare than the bow, and no turnout flare to the gunwales. They were large ceremonial canoes and were usually elaborately painted. They traveled well but were hard to maneuver in turns.

A relative of the head canoe, the spruce or Sitka canoe (*seet yaakw* in Tlingit), was used up until the twentieth century. [35] These were typical northern canoes of the nineteenth century. They tended to be smaller boats, employed for everyday use. They had small, thin extensions for the bow and stern projections.

Closely related were the cottonwood canoes made by Tlingit groups who lived along rivers in the northern part of the Panhandle, such as the people of Klukwan.

The classic northern-style canoe, which is represented in this project, improved upon the earlier styles by the addition of an overhanging, upswept bow and stern which created a more sturdy craft with a very dramatic profile. These canoes had efficient cutwaters which allowed more maneuverability, especially in the wind.

All of these canoes were propelled with single-bladed paddles, poles and/or sails.

Canoes were accorded great respect for their life-giving function and took on important spiritual significance. Paul Jackson Sr. explains his culture's connection to respect and how that relates to the high esteem in which canoes were held:

Spiritual Significance

The Tlingit nation watched. They watched animals, birds and fish. And that's where they arrived at these things we use and are trying to pass on today. One of these values is the respect for all things, living and dead. Just because something dies doesn't mean you no longer respect it. We don't shoot animals to hang their heads on the wall. We don't fish streams until the fish are no longer there. We don't chop down trees until there are no longer trees there.

We call the trees "the tree people," *aas ḵwáani.* The trees are a living thing just like we are, and they deserve to live just like us. And so when we cut down a tree, we are killing one of their people. There is a tree ceremony. When we have this ceremony, we are asking for forgiveness from the *aas ḵwaani* for taking one of them. We do not waste that tree. We tell the tree people that we are going to make a canoe out of the tree. This canoe will do a great thing for our people, bring food or transport us.

The last canoe that was made here in Sitka was made to feed the mind. That's because we are going to use it to educate not only our people, but also other people, about the way our people live.

We do not cut down trees and waste them. We do not waste anything. We have respect for all things. The way the Tlingit people arrived at this respect is:

A Tlingit hunter walking in the woods. He decided to sit down and rest. As he sat down, there was an egg on the ground. He watched it. He saw a little bird trying to get out of its shell. When the little bird got out of the shell, it ran around and looked at all the holes in the stumps. The man was curious. That little bird found a hole he liked,

cleaned that hole out and then went and got some moss, some clean moss, and he went and put that in the hole. Then he took the shell that protected him and put it into the hole, and then more moss.

What this little bird was doing, was taking the shell that protected him until he was old enough to get out in the world on his own, and put it out of harm's way. He knew if he left it out, an animal would come by and step on the shell and break it. We call this haa daakanóox'u, *our ancestors: our outer shell that protects us until we are ready to go out into the world on our own. So like the little bird, we respect our grandparents and our ancestors, the respect for all things.*

That tree that is going to be chopped down and become a canoe, we give it a name. There is a ceremony that is held and a name is given, just like with a human being when it is born. When this canoe is no longer of any use and it starts to rot, we don't leave it on the beach and let it break up. We get the opposite moiety and we have them break up the canoe and we cremate it, much like you would a human being. This is out of respect for that tree. There is a tree that is used for a canoe, which is a red cedar.

A long time ago there was a young lady, a daughter of a leader, who gave birth to a red cedar branch. The leader didn't know what to do about it so he called the other leaders in the village together and told them what happened, "There is a branch, a red cedar branch. What do we do with it?"

The leader's grandson was there and, like all little boys, he was playing out by the door and making a lot of noise. Pretty soon his grandpa hollered at him and said, "Will you be quiet out there! We have these great leaders here trying to figure out what to do about this branch and you're disturbing us." The little boy kept quiet for a while. But like all little boys, he was soon back to making noise again.

So his grandpa called him in. "You see all these people? These are all the big shots in the village. We have

Chief Shake's Brown Bear Haida canoe with twenty-five passengers
coming into the clan house on Shakes Island in Wrangell.

Anchorage Museum B80.108.14

Haida canoe, gift to Governor Brady from Chief Sonihat
of Kasaan, 1904. Photo taken in Sitka, Alaska.

this problem. We have this branch and we're trying to decide what to do with it." The little boy thought and said, "Why don't you take it up on the hill and plant it where the sun shines on it." The little boy solved their problem. They took it up there and planted it. That tree grew into a red cedar. So the red cedar became the grandchild of the Tlingit people. If you cut the red cedar, it has the same color as the human flesh. In a storm, if you crawl under there, the branches will protect you. Also we are told that sometimes it is good to listen to your children. You can't always just tell them what to do.

The carvers in the past were the most educated people in our Tlingit nation, in all the nations. They were the most educated in the traditional way, the reason being that when a decision is made to build a canoe, the word is put out by the clan that is going to make the canoe. They bring in a *naa káani* from the other moiety and tell him what they want to do.[36] And then that man is sent out to get a carver. A carver is brought in and then the history of that clan is told to the carver. The carver listens to these different stories, and from that he draws the designs. That is the reason we say the carvers are the most educated in our traditional way. They are next to the historians, the leaders who tell these stories to them, but the carvers have all the history from all the different people. So the carver is very important.

It is important to know that it is always the opposite moiety that is hired to do it. It's not that we don't know how to do it, but there is a reason for it. If we do it ourselves, it is worth only what we put into it, the price of the material. When we do it the traditional way, when we get the opposite moiety to do it, it takes on a different value. We pay the other people to do it and it is brought out traditionally. There are witnesses that are invited to witness what is going on. There are gifts that are given so people can remember what went on.

Many of the things that our people did in the past were almost lost completely, taken away from us, taken away from our ancestors. It was against the law to sing and dance, to speak our language, to do the things that we normally do. The whole idea behind this was that if we no longer spoke our language, did the things that we do and lost our history, we no longer exist as a nation. In 1904 in Sitka, there was an order given to the Tlingit nation that they would have their last party (potlatch) here in Sitka and then there would be no more parties given after that. [37]

So the word went out, and the people from all over Southeast Alaska came and had the party here. Our ancestors, being very wise, saw what was happening. So they said, "We will send our children to their schools so they can learn the ways of the white man, and in the future they will speak on our behalf. But there will be families among us who will continue doing the things we do now. And sometime in the future, these people will become teachers to our own people." That is what is happening now. We have come to the point where we have become teachers to our people. Many of our people don't understand why we do these things.

The canoe, to our people, is very important. The Tlingit nation did not make the big canoes. It was the Haidas. They had the great big red cedars and they were the ones that built the big canoes which the white man calls war canoes. They were not built for war; they were built for transporting people out in the ocean. They were called *Lukadawóox'* which means "broad nose." Up on the bow there is a platform where a man stands when they are coming in to shore and the challenge is issued from the beach, "*Goodáx yaakw sáyá*," which means, "Where are these boats from?" This is our protocol. Even though you have invited them, this is the protocol you have to use. The boats will not come ashore until they are invited. On the canoe, there will be a person to respond. They will say, for instance, "We are the boats from Juneau." Then the man on the beach will say, "Welcome, welcome, come on ashore. Over here is a good place to land your boat. There is good sand there. Come ashore and share some water with us."

This is the protocol that we go through. It's out of respect for each other. The respect is there at all times.[38]

Northwest Coast Dugout Canoe, Northern Style

Against The Wind, Xoon yee aadé
Cultures Represented: Tlingit, Haida, Tsimshian, Eyak

Length: 19′   Width: 41″   Depth: 50″   Weight: 200 lbs.
Materials: Red cedar, pigment

Master boat builder: Wayne Price, Haines, Alaska
Apprentice: Vanessa Pazar
Paddle carver: Warren Price

Early in the nineteenth century, canoes of this type with raised sterns and bows came into use. They are called "broad nose" or "the northern style."

These canoes sometimes had an additional plank applied to the gunwales to allow them to carry more, and used square-rigged sails of woven mats for running downwind. These craft would often reach sixty feet, have up to two masts and sails, and could carry as much as eight tons of freight. The wealthiest Northwest Coast people purchased these magnificent craft from the Haidas, who were acknowledged as master canoe builders. Names would be given to the canoes and crest designs would be carved or painted upon them to show ownership.

This dugout canoe is the only boat in the Heritage Center's project that employs a reductive method of construction. Following ancient techniques, the boat was given form through the hollowing-out and careful shaping of a red cedar log. The only additions to the craft are the bow and stern pieces, thwarts and gunwale rails. A small detachable mast and sail are provided along with the paddles.

The canoe was steamed open, so its width became more than that of the tree from which it was carved. This adds stability to the craft. Hot lava rocks were placed into the salt water filling the canoe cavity. Spreaders were used to gradually push the sides outward. The steaming also produced the results of the

Wayne Price and apprentice Vanessa Pazar rest on the
canoe log. Wayne is holding a model canoe he carved and
steamed open just as is done with the full-size canoes.

The tree ceremony reenacted by members of the Tlingit nation. The ceremony is performed with great respect to ask permission of the *aas kwaani* or "tree people" to take one of their members in order to make a canoe or totem pole.

bottom flattening and the bow and stern lifting up. This part of the canoe-making process is one which always draws a crowd to watch the somewhat "magical" transformation of raw wood by steam. The steaming for *Against the Wind* took place in August at the village of Eklutna with the Denaina Tribe as hosts.

In order to prepare for the ceremony, Wayne fasted according to tradition. During the steaming, he added the heartwood that had been taken from the log to the top of the fire that was heating the rocks. This was done, according to him, in order to "put life back into the log."

Against the Wind derives its name from the fact the craft's construction was accomplished in a non-traditional manner. Breaking with tradition, a female apprentice was used.

> *I can definitely say we work good together. I didn't know how it was actually going to work. I had a lot of deep thought when I first started this canoe. The women were not allowed on dugout canoes. I think the research says it was because of fertility. A long time ago they kept the woman separate from the implements that killed because the canoe was used in hunting. Women gave birth, they actually gave life, and the ship would be involved in taking life; they were kept separate. I don't know how big of a can of worms I've opened up but the canoe steamed open really good and it floats great. I said, "Okay, well we're going to break the rules and by golly we're going to do it standing up."* — Wayne Price

Visitors to the carving site couldn't help but be impressed by the enthusiasm and hard work the seventeen-year-old apprentice exhibited day after day. It was as though she was driven to be the best and reinforce Wayne's confidence in her. Her dedication and skill exhibited that there is a place in this activity for women, even though the concept is non-traditional to Native culture. A little competition entered into the long days of hard work as Vanessa said playfully, "Oh, it's the only way to keep in there and give Wayne a run for his money."

Warren Price, Wayne's son, was at the site for part of the summer. He carved all of the paddles and worked on the canoe. He also answered questions and handed out the fragrant cedar chips from the canoe log to the visitors. The smell of the cedar at a carving site always captivates the visitors. It has a refreshing scent, one that people are fortunate to experience. As with current logging practices, cedar is becoming a rare material.

WAYNE PRICE

I'm a Tlingit. I was born in Juneau, 1957, and I grew up in Haines. My Indian name is Ian.xí. It is the first flower that grows on a new mountain. My other Indian name is actually Xóotk' and that's Little Bear. I'm a Wooshkeetaan, a Shark, a Thunderbird, Eagle, and Wolf from Kake, Alaska.

Against the Wind is a Haida-style canoe in honor of their great ocean-going craft. I really love their style. It's the hardest style of canoe and has been carved by a Tlingit. The Haida-style canoe has a cutwater in the bow. To represent all four tribes, we have an Eyak paddle, a Tlingit paddle, a Haida paddle, and a Tsimshian paddle in the canoe so that all four tribes are represented equally.

A long time ago, they used to have great ceremonies when one village would travel to another village. There would be great feasting and dancing and the canoes were all a big part of that. I don't think that part of the culture should ever pass on or be left behind.

Canoes were such an important part of our life. They used them for gathering food and transportation from one village to next. They were an intregal part of our life for not only the Tlingit, but Haidas, Tsimshian and Eyaks as well. I feel this is like the very pinnacle in doing any kind of woodwork considering all the technology that it takes to create an ocean-going craft like they used a long time ago. If you think you're very good, try a canoe and you'll find out exactly whether you are or not.

This is the fifth canoe I've been involved with and I'm still learning. Every log I've been on is very different. I got started when I was carving a lot of totem poles in Southeast. I was working with Steve Brown down in Wrangell. We were working on the Chief Shakes house posts. He told me that he'd done canoes in Neah Bay, and my curiosity was really awakened. He gave a model canoe-carving class in Ketchikan.

I took that little canoe-carving class and we actually had a chance to carve it all the way to specs and actually steam it. You steam the little guys. It turned out to be a whole lot of fun and I was really inspired from that. I went to Wrangell and actually found out where the old-timers had picked their trees from. I went and I picked a tree. That's the one that I took up to Chilkoot Culture Camp in Haines, back around '82. It was actually my first attempt at carving a canoe and it led to helping Steve with a forty-foot down in Discovery Park in Seattle. We were not able to complete that one but it sure was a lot of work. Now this is the fifth one that I've been involved with and I'm still learning about the dugout canoe.

Clan House
I became involved in this canoe project as a result of a cosmetic job I did on the clan house at Site Five at the Alaska Native Heritage Center. Then I started on the entrance pole. It took me four days to dig the hole in the front and it took thirty days to make the pole. As soon as the pole went into place my boss handed me the cell phone and the keys and said, "Here. I gotta go. You can be the boss."

So the next day I had a crew of seven guys working under me and I had to build a clan house! Not knowing anything about building a clan house, I just kinda rolled up my sleeves and went for it, just took each project at a time. I paired off my crew to see who could work together and, by golly, we built the clan house. It took us about three months. I got my crew off the roof two days before it snowed. It was an incredible experience.

Apprentice
I got the bid early last spring to do the canoe and moved here from Haines for the summer. I chose Vanessa Pazar as my apprentice. I had three other guys that were supposed to be along with me. None of them really ever worked out and Vanessa was the last person left standing, so I chose her. She didn't know anything about carving a canoe, but I knew she was a real hard worker.

Blessing the Log
We had Major Murray from the Salvation Army come up here and bless the log. By that time we were starting to make our adzes. We made our blades from the leaf springs out of a dump truck. They're thicker, wider, longer and heavier than all previous adzes that I've ever used. The reason I did that was the old, "heavier hammer" theory. "If you've got a bigger hammer you can make a bigger chip."

Left: Wayne Price uses his adz to shape the exterior of the canoe while his son Warren watches. Above: After the exterior is completed, the canoe is flipped and Wayne begins the process of hollowing the interior.

Getting Down to Work

So then we took the log and loaded it up on a flatbed and we took it over to Lake Hood. We floated the log in the lake so we could find our centerline. When the log settled down, stopped rocking back and forth, that's where I drew my centerline and that was the centerline of the canoe.

We brought it back over to the Heritage Center. The first cut I made was the very bottom cut. On the bottom of the boat, it had a dip in it of two inches that gave me my center line, so we popped the centerline and with that I was able to measure out anywhere from center on either side of the ship, to start carving the shape of the canoe.

Steaming the canoe open. Five-gallon buckets of salt water stand by, waiting to be poured into the canoe. Hot lava rocks are then added to create steam. The steam transforms the wood by making it soft and pliable. The sides of the canoe are forced out, the bottom drops and the bow and stern rise up. The steaming took place north of Anchorage at Eklutna with the members of the Eklutna tribe as hosts.

112

I used what I call the "plank" theory. You just take a bevel on each side, making a plank. We took our ship adzes and adzed all that material off until it was perfectly flat. By that time we both were just learning how to adz and getting into shape. The first week is getting all broken in – slept good at night.

We used that plank theory on the whole ship. I just ran planks the full twenty feet and I ran a bevel so when I got the first two planks done, then I moved onto the next two and they were pitched a little more. We ran them the full twenty feet. So each step of this canoe has to be done completely in order to get to the next step. We did the planks and planked all the way out to the gunwales and we brought the log over to the carving shed and I hooked up my Alaskan chainsaw. Then I put the bendy boards on the log and that's how I got the outside line of the gunwales. I could tell by the bulk of the material of the log that we could hook up a chainsaw mill to my chainsaw.

We rolled the log on its side so the canoe was actually laying sideways and hooked up the Alaskan mill and ran a long plank two inches until we got amidship of the boat. We planked down the next one so that when we were all done it looked like steps. That was how we got the material off the four corners of the ship. After we had all four corners planked we took the ship adzes and we adzed right down to the gunwales.

Then Vanessa and I took out our Stanley block planes and planed the whole thing all the way smooth. We did two sides. We used the handy-man jack to roll the log over and did it on the other side, got that all done, then we rolled it so it was upside-down. We shot our keel line so that the keel was one inch thick on bow and stern. That helped us know the rest of the material we had to dig away. That's when the adzing began.

We started chopping on her and first thing we noticed is that the blades were a lot tougher than the adz handles. We smashed four or five handles in the first week. We had to go out and make more handles. I decided I had gone a little bit big on the old adz but

after a few weeks you break into it. I picked up the elbow adz that I adzed the totem pole in Sitka with and seemed just like a little toy. It was like a feather!

So we shaped the whole outside of the boat and we still used the bendy board plank theory. After I got the outside all shaped the way that I wanted, it looked exactly like it was a planked wooden boat. I didn't cut the cutwater or stern line yet.

I think it was about a month or so into that we were able to finally take all the plank lines off and make it look like a ship.

Then I cut the cutwater and the stern line in and we put the gunwale lines on and had it all shaped. We got all the lumps out, all the puffs out. We'd look at it, circle puffs, adz it again and take the puff out until I was happy.

When I was happy where it was, I took the big adz that I made and I detail adzed the whole outside of the ship.

Then we started drilling it full of holes. I had quarter-inch dowels. I went the span of my hand lengthwise and five inches wide from bottom to top. I put these pegs in. I made the drill holes seven-thirty-seconds inch which is just a little bit smaller than a quarter inch. So when I pounded the dowels in they would be sound and they wouldn't come back out. It looked like a completely finished boat.

Next, we turned it back over, right-side-up, and it was a tree again! Still had the bark on it. We started all over.

We hooked up my Alaska chain saw mill. The gunwale sweep, which is the gunwale line – all that material between there – we did the same thing. We made a notch just enough so I could do a two-inch plank and stick my chain saw mill in there, and we ran the whole length of the boat. That gave us our first step. Then we made another notch, enough to get the chain saw in there and ran another plank all the way up from gunwale to gunwale. We got all that material out of there in one day. I used the boards that we made for paddles and the seats. We also made small paddles for gifts for when we dedicated *Against the Wind*.

So we took all that material off, planed the whole top of my ship smooth so we could even up the gunwales. It's really hard to get them real accurate when it's a tree. They needed a little tuning up. We leveled the log so it was perfectly level. Once it was level all the way across, I knew my gunwales were the same. We shot the inside gunwale lines. I think we measured it two inches.

We took out the big chain saw again with the three-foot bar on it instead of the forty-two-inch bar, and I did some freehand saw cuts that were just phenomenal. The saw, I maxed it out, made some impossible cuts with it. I just got up on the log and did it before I knew it was impossible. I flipped the chain once, but that's okay. When you're making cuts like that, there's a lot that can go wrong. We've been really lucky. I made those cuts, took out the ship adzes again, and I told Vanessa, "Well, somewhere inside this log you're going to learn how to adz."

We were on a rock-solid schedule of ten, twelve hours a day, seven days a week. That was day sixty and we had only had two days off. We got the inside hollowed out in exactly eight days. Took us four days to get to the first peg which I think is really remarkable.

After the inside is all shaped and we got everything where I wanted, we lightened up the stern and worked on plugging all the knots.

She was a solid log but had a heart crack. She's a good log, just a couple of bad knots on the side. I was able to patch those. Then we made the gunwales, and the seats. Then we rigged it for a sail. We had a sail custom-made just like in old pictures but out of canvas. The mast is right up front. She is rigged for three or four people.

Steaming

We steamed her on August 23 up in Eklutna. It took a whole day. George Bennett brought about a thousand pounds of lava rocks from Sitka for the steaming. We used salt water, put it inside the canoe with hot lava rocks to make the steam. We gained eight inches in the width of the canoe and six inches in the height of the bow and stern.

The Future

Vanessa, my apprentice, is a hard worker. We did ten to twelve hours a day on a regular basis and we only had two days off in sixty days. She kept up really good. I'm really proud of her. I'm pretty sure Vanessa will be involved with me on a future project, probably a totem or something.

It's getting hard to get the big trees for projects like this. I sure hope they're saving a few patches here and there. I'm having to do more and more repairs every time I do a canoe. There is more and more bad core wood. I'm sure learning how to make good patches.

I hope that what I'm doing, and the documentation that's being done on the *Against the Wind*, can be my way of expressing the need for keeping this alive, keep it going. It's such an important part of our history, our tradition, that it should not be lost. Any person that ever does one is really going to find out that it's a real lot of work. Our people had to work very hard just to be able to go out and go fishing and hunting. A lot of the modern tools that we have today just don't even work on a dugout canoe. It has its own language and it demands a lot of attention. Once you start one, you should never ever put it down until it's done, just as in the days of old. It's become a very big part of my life.

Being involved with the Alaska Native Heritage Center has been a great learning experience for me, and the first time I've been able to be around these other nifty kinds of boats that are being made, and all the other boat builders. It's really nice to watch these boats being done. It's just super fantastic, seeing all eight boats in the water. Never been done before!

VANESSA PAZAR

As the apprentice on this canoe, I've learned just about everything I can. I tried to soak up all the knowledge. The strange thing is, most of the stuff I learned, I wasn't told. I just learned how to stand back and watch and learn that way. I think that's the best way for me. It was the way I was raised up, so it comes natural. And the way Wayne is the teacher and master carver, it works real well. We've turned into quite a team.

I was born in Bellingham, Washington, but I think I moved to Alaska when I was three. I'm seventeen years old. My Tlingit name is Kaalkéis'. I'm from the Kaagwaantaan clan, Eagle/Wolf.

When I was growing up I took language and dance classes. My mom thought it was really important, since I was adopted, to keep in touch with my heritage. I am so glad. It makes me the person I am today. If I hadn't grown up around fish camp and language and dancing classes, I would've been a totally different person. I wouldn't have learned the lessons I have and the respect I have for nature and elders. I have done woodworking all my life, but this is my first carving project. I love it! It's in the blood. There is a lot of hard work in doing this. When I think of the traditional ways, sometimes I just have to sit back go, "Whoa, they did this with stone tools." Oh boy! I have a lot of dedication but that might have been doing a little too much. I don't know, it's a lot of hard work, but at the end of the day when you're all sore and tired, you know you've worked for it. You've earned it.

We put in about ten hours a day, seven days a week. Some days, it was twelve hours a day. We had eleven to twelve full garbage bags of chips in about five or six days when we were really blasting. Then we slowed down and did a lot of the fine-tuning. Wayne had to work on the patches that we had to do for the bow and the stern and we had a couple of knothole patches. Then we made a mast for the sail.

The log was beautiful on the inside. It did have a heart crack all the way through it, but that didn't really slow us down. We keep it wet all day long to keep it from cracking. At night we put a burlap over it and then we wet her down. Super soaker!

The name "Against the Wind" came from one day we were riding our bikes to the center and the wind was blowing hard, right in our faces. It was difficult to pedal. I said, "Man, we're going against the wind." Wayne answered, "That's the name of the boat!"

I think this is going to carry on. I think it's just starting to begin, I really do. I'm the first female canoe carver for this style and I get to see thousands of females come to this place every day and every one of them is gung-ho for it. So I know there is going to be some future women canoe carvers out there. Women were generally never allowed near the canoe unless it was already built. It was considered a bad omen, I believe. I just think if you're a hard worker and you have dedication and you just like wood carving, then you should definitely look into it. It gives you a feeling of peace that you've never really felt before.

Previous page: *Against the Wind* with its crew during the launching
ceremony off Homer. Bow to stern: Wayne Price (in cedar hat),
George and James Bennett, Margaret Nelson and Vanessa Pazar.
Above: As the sail is hoisted and catches the wind, Wayne raises his
paddle in a gesture of triumph.

Notes

1. The return of the beaver prow figure was arranged under NAGPRA (Native American Graves Protection and Repatriation Act) which provides for the return of items to tribal groups deemed to be the rightful owners. The act was signed into law by President Bush in 1991 and addresses objects of cultural patrimony, human remains and associated funerary objects.

2. Zimmerly, 1986, pg. 3.

3. Fitzhugh and Kaplan, 1982, pg. 60.

4. Adney and Chapelle, 1983, pg. 7.

5. Refer to Salmon interview beginning pg. 8.

6. The Kaax'achgook story belongs to the Kiks'adi clan. In order to hear it told in its entirety, one must ask a person of that clan.

7. Riehle, Jim, 1996.

8. Refer to Kawagley interview, Introduction to Kayaks, beginning pg. 30.

9. As told to the editor in an interview conducted summer 2000.

10. Neel, 1995, pg.3.

11. Ibid, pg. 2.

12. Huntington, 1993, pg. 52-53.

13. As told to the editor in an interview conducted summer 2000.

14. Babiche, or rawhide, is made from a skin of an animal (usually caribou or moose) that has been fleshed and the hair removed. The skin is worked wet. It is cut from the skin in a circular motion in order to get the maximum amount of length to each piece. Babiche is used to lash kayaks, canoes, snowshoes and sleds.

15. Zimmerly, 1986, pg.3.

16. As told to the editor in an interview conducted summer 2000.

17. Ray, 1981, pg. 42.

18. Interview conducted with June Simeonoff Pardue by the editor, summer 2000.

19. A *qasegiq* is a men's house where men would eat, sleep, take sweat baths, play games and work on hunting gear. Sometimes it would become a community house for meetings and a place where important ceremonies would take place. They were semi-subterranean with a fire pit and a smoke hole above.

20. Interview conducted by the editor with Oscar Kawagley summer 2000.

21. The term "Kwig" is an accepted shortened version of the Yup'ik placename Kwigillingok.

Notes

22. An *altatl* is a throwing board which is used to add leverage when throwing a dart or a spear.

23. The term *Alutiiq* refers to the group of people whose traditional homelands include Prince William Sound, the outer Kenai Peninsula, the Kodiak Archipelago and the Alaska Peninsula. They are also referred to as *Sugpiaq*.

24. Larry Matfay was a teacher of Alutiiq culture. He traveled extensively giving talks and conducting classes. He was also a kayak builder. In the mid-1990s he built a kayak for the Native Art Center at University of Alaska, Fairbanks. He passed away in 1998.

25. The Yup'ik tradition of enclosing grass into seams makes gut or skin seams watertight when they get wet. The grass soaks up water and swells the seams shut.

26. "Paddle to Seattle" took place in 1989 to commemorate Washington State's 100th anniversary.

27. *The Starship and the Canoe*, Kenneth Brower, Harper and Row, 1979.

28. Braund, 1988, pg. 21.

29. Silook, 1976, pg. 1.

30. The Alaska Eskimo Whaling Commission was formed in 1977 to represent whaling communities and coordinate with agencies responsible for the management of subsistence whaling.

31. Braund, 1988, pg. 25-29.

32. *Muktuk* is whale blubber, or fat, considered a delicacy among whale-hunting communities of Alaska.

33. As told to the editor in an interview conducted summer 2000.

34. Corey, 1987, "The Head Canoe," Bill Holm, pg. 143-155.

35. Lecture given by Steve Brown in Sitka, November 2000.

36. In Tlingit culture, a *naa káani* is a person chosen to conduct an event, mediate or give advice. Traditionally, this would be the highest ranking in-law married into the clan, thus of the opposite moiety. This person is usually very knowledgeable in traditional, cultural ways including protocol. Moiety refers to two major divisions. In Tlingit culture, these are Eagle and Raven (traditionally Wolf and Raven). Within each of these are many clans and houses.

37. In 1904, Governor Brady of Alaska announced there would be one last potlatch to be held in Sitka and after that, potlatches were to be banned. It was a large occasion with people coming in canoes from all parts of southeast Alaska.

38. Interview conducted by the editor with Paul Jackson, summer 2000.

Glossary

Angyapik – A Siberian Yupik open skin boat similar to the umiak.

Baidarka (sing.) *Baidarki* (pl.) – Russian word for kayak.

Bifid or bifurcated bow – Forked or two-part bow.

Bow – The forward part of a boat or ship.

Canoe – An open, double-ended boat with little or no deck covering.

Cockpit – An opening in the deck of a boat where a person sits (also see *Hatch*).

Coaming – A raised frame around a cockpit or hatch to keep the water out.

Deck – Top covering of a boat.

Draft – The depth of a boat in the water.

Dugout canoe – A boat made by hollowing out a large log.

Frame – The construction system of a boat that gives shape or strength; a skeleton not filled in or covered.

Gunwale – The upper edge of a boat's side.

Hatch – An opening in the deck of a boat where a person sits (also see *Cockpit*).

Kayak – A small watercraft made of a covered frame except for a small opening or openings in the deck to accommodate paddlers and passengers.

Keel – A longitudinal timber or plate extending along the center of the bottom of a ship and often projecting from the bottom.

Keelson – A longitudinal structure running above and fastened to the keel of a ship in order to stiffen and strengthen its framework.

Qayaq – Yup'ik word for kayak.

Qasegiq – Men's ceremonial house (Yup'ik).

Red ochre – An earthy and often impure iron ore used as a pigment and preservative.

Rib – A traverse member of a frame that runs from keel to deck.

Stern – The rear end of a boat.

Stringer – A long horizontal timber to connect uprights in a frame or to support a frame.

Strut – A structural piece designed to resist pressure in the direction of its length.

Thwart – A structural piece placed across or athwart a boat.

Umiak – An Iñupiat open skin-covered boat with a wooden frame similar to the *angyapik*.

References

Adney, Edward Tappan and Chapelle, Howard I.
1983 THE BARK CANOES AND SKIN BOATS OF
NORTH AMERICA
Smithsonian Institution Press, Washington D.C.

Braund, Stephen R.
1986 THE SKIN BOATS OF ST. LAWRENCE ISLAND,
ALASKA
University of Washington Press, Seattle and London.

Corey, Peter L.
1987 FACES, VOICES AND DREAMS: A CELEBRATION
OF THE CENTENNIAL OF SHELDON JACKSON
MUSEUM
Division of Alaska State Museums and Friends of the Alaska
State Museum, Juneau.

Dart, Joe
1981 ALASKANS HOW-TO HANDBOOK
Interior Trappers Association, Fairbanks.

Dyson, George
1988 BAIDARKA: THE KAYAK.
Alaska Northwest Books, Anchorage, Seattle, Portland.

Fitzhugh, William W. and Kaplan, Susan A.
1982 INUA: SPIRIT WORLD OF THE BERING SEA
ESKIMO
Smithsonian Institution Press, Washington D.C.

Huntington, Sydney (as told to Jim Rearden)
1993 SHADOWS ON THE KOYUKUK: AN ALASKAN
NATIVE'S LIFE ALONG THE RIVER
Alaska Northwest Books, Anchorage, Seattle and Portland.

Jacobsen, Johan Adrian (translated by Erna Gunther)
1995 ALASKA VOYAGES 1881-1883: AN EXPEDITION
TO THE NORTHWEST COAST OF AMERICA
The University of Chicago Press, Chicago and London.

Neel, David
1996 THE GREAT CANOES: REVIVING A
NORTHWEST COAST TRADITION
Douglas & McIntyre, Vancouver and Toronto,
University of Washington Press, Seattle.

Ray, Dorothy Jean
1981 ALEUT AND ESKIMO ART: TRADITION AND
INNOVATION IN SOUTH ALASKA
University of Washington Press, Seattle.

Silook, Roger S.
1976 SEEVOOKUK: STORIES THE OLD PEOPLE
TOLD ON ST. LAWRENCE ISLAND
Published by author.

Snaith, Skip
1977 UMIAK: AN ILLUSTRATED GUIDE
Walrose and Hyde, Eastsound, Washington.

Stewart, Hilary
1983 CEDAR
Douglas & McIntyre, Vancouver and Toronto,
University of Washington Press, Seattle and London.

Vick, Ann
1984 THE CAMA-I BOOK
Anchor Press, Doubleday, Garden City, New York.

Wickersham, James
1938 JUDGE WICKERSHAM'S OLD YUKON
Washington Law Book Co., Washington D.C.

Zimmerly, David W.
1986 QAYAQ: KAYAKS OF SIBERIA AND ALASKA
Alaska State Museum, Division of State Museums,
Department of Education, Juneau, Alaska.

2000 HOOPER BAY KAYAK CONSTRUCTION
Canadian Museum of Civilization.

Acknowledgments

*Special thanks go to the following who greatly assisted in
taking this project and book from a vision to a reality.*

Funding: Rockefeller Foundation, Save America's Treasures
and Alaska Native Heritage Center.

The boat builders, their apprentices, skin and root sewers and families,
Vernon Chimegalrea, Alexis Bunten, Cindy Pennington, Margaret Nelson,
Paul M. Jackson Sr. (research and storytelling), Robin Klanott (transcriptions),
Bob Jenkins and Nerland Agency, Kelly Ketchum (editing), Chris Boyd, Mike Gifford,
Susan Elliott (proofreader), Greg Epkes (map art), Harold Jacobs, Roby Littlefield,
Stephan and Kassandra Eubank, Teresa Moses, Norman Kohler, Nels Lawson Jr.,
Jimmy George, Kaadulsh̲k̲xi yis (Sitka Canoe Club), Nels Lawson Sr.,
Howard Luke, Oscar Kawagley, Village of Eklutna, George Bennett and family,
the village site interpreters at Alaska Native Heritage Center, Pratt Museum, Qayanek,
Britt and Charlie Sandberg, Dan and Michelle Ketchum, Steve Brown.

A special thank you to Paul Jackson Sr. whose Tlingit wisdom gave me guidance
in this project and to the other Alaska Native elders who have been
my teachers and guides throughout the years:

Austin Hammond, Sarah Malcolm, Judson Brown, Howard Luke, Rita Blumenstein,
Sally Hudson, Lillian Hammond, Cecilia Kunz.

Dedication

*This book is dedicated to all of the boat builders
in this project and to their ancestors who had the
patience, wisdom and skill to build seaworthy craft
from the few natural materials they had
available in their environment, and then venture
fearlessly out onto some of the roughest seas in the
world to gather sustenance for their families.*